IN PALLISER·S TRIANGLE
Living in the Grasslands
1850–1930

Barry Potyondi

Purich Publishing

Saskatoon, Saskatchewan

Canada

Published by Purich Publishing in cooperation with Parks Canada—Department of Canadian Heritage and the Canada Communications Group—Publishing, Department of Supply and Services Canada.

The publisher also gratefully acknowledges the contribution of Canadian Heritage—Parks Canada, Grasslands National Park, towards the publication of this book.

Purich Publishing
Box 23032, Market Mall Post Office
Saskatoon, SK
Canada S7J 5H3

Canadian Cataloguing in Publication Data

Potyondi, Barry, 1954–

In Palliser's Triangle

ISBN 1–895830–06–0

1. Grassland ecology - Saskatchewan - History.
2. Grasslands - Saskatchewan - Effect of man on - History. 3. Habitat (Ecology) - Modification - Saskatchewan - History. 4. Man - Influence on nature - Saskatchewan. I. Title.

QH541.5.P7P67 1995 574.5'2643'0971243 C95–920219–6

Editing, design, and layout by Jane McHughen Publishing Services, Saskatoon, Saskatchewan
Cover design and photo layout by NEXT Communications, Inc., Saskatoon, Saskatchewan
Cover photograph by John Perret, Saskatoon, Saskatchewan
Printed in Canada by Kromar Printing Ltd., Winnipeg, Manitoba
Printed on acid-free paper

The cover photograph illustrates the rolling grasslands of southern Saskatchewan. The photograph was taken to the north and east of the Grasslands National Park, East Block boundary.

CONTENTS

Map on page 10; illustrations follow page 74

Acknowledgments

This book began as a federal government study of environmental change in the two small blocks of land (some 350 square miles/900 km^2) that make up Grasslands National Park, situated near the international boundary in southwestern Saskatchewan. The work exists only because of the foresight of several Parks Canada representatives who have long held that we need historical studies to underpin environmental management in our national parks system. I am thinking particularly of Dr. Richard Stuart, formerly chief of historical research with the Prairie and Northern Regional Office of Parks Canada at Winnipeg, and Jim Masyk and Keith W. Foster, superintendent and chief park warden, respectively, of Grasslands National Park. Their support for this project was always strong, their observations acute, their intent unwavering. I am fortunate to have worked with them.

Many others contributed significantly to the project research and analysis. I am particularly indebted to David Gauthier, Randy Widdis, Marilyn Lewry, Margaret Carter, Thelma Poirier, and Lisa Dale for their assistance and critical commentary. I join with them in extending our heartfelt thanks to the many archivists and librarians across the country who steered us in the direction of profitable sources on a subject that defies every convention of the Standard Classification System.

I must also thank Don Purich of Purich Publishing and Jane McHughen of Jane McHughen Publishing Services for gently shepherding the manuscript on its journey toward a more general readership. Don's enthusiasm is infectious and his perseverance admirable. He alone can claim credit for overcoming numerous obstacles to publication. For her part, Jane taught me more than a thing or two about writing. Until her pencil scythed through my tangle of prose, I had no idea professional editing could be so humbling and exhilarating at the same time. The least I can do is to acknowledge her ever-present if invisible hand in the work that follows.

As always, my greatest appreciation goes to my family—Teresa, Stephen, and Matthew—who could not be more understanding about the demands of the written word.

INTRODUCTION
The Changing Look of the Land

Environment may initially shape the range of choices available to a people .
. . but then culture reshapes the environment in responding to those choices.[1]
William Cronon

When settlers first came to southwestern Saskatchewan, around 1908, they marveled at the tall grass that grew profusely. "Stirrup-high" was how many described it; others said it was "knee-high on the cows."[2] Yet with the arrival of Euro-Canadian farmers, the tall grass vanished as quickly as had the vast herds of buffalo that grazed the plains for millennia. The loss of the native grasslands represents the momentous changes that people have made to the plains environment. It is but one sign of a relentless process that we can trace from the time Native Peoples last hunted buffalo on the plains to the present day.

I grew up in rural Saskatchewan and to my young eyes the land seemed changeless. Each spring brought more scampering gophers to hunt in sun-drenched pastures, more pussy willows to gather in tangles of sheltering bush, more slippery frogs to chase at the margins of countless sloughs. Looking back with the perspective of several decades, however, I now remember just as vividly the volunteer gangs of neighbors clear-cutting rights of way through the bush for an ambitious municipal road construction program. I recall the annual visits of contract bulldozer operators who flattened stands of poplar trees on one farm after another, then pushed them into huge windrows to be burnt. I can still picture the gargantuan farm equipment, bought on the strength of federal farm subsidies, that tore up the slough bottoms to make them "productive" and, like mechanical glaciers, resculpted the grassy hills where I went sledding every winter. As the images suggest, I grew up in Saskatchewan's parkland, a region more favored by soils and climate than the semi-arid country considered in this book. Yet the point is the same: environmental change has been a constant in the history of Canada's West.

Southwestern Saskatchewan is, in many ways, the perfect test plot for this kind of historical investigation. Bounded more or less by the Missouri Coteau on the east, the Cypress Hills on the west, the 49th parallel on the south, and the Canadian Pacific Railway's main line on the north, it is a lonely, parched landscape of rolling hills and sun-cured grass. Between 1850 and 1908, it was home successively to Native Peoples, Métis, and cattle ranchers, each of whom understood and used the local resources very differently. Farmers began to arrive in 1908. The most marginal croplands of southwestern Saskatchewan, situated in and around today's Grasslands National Park, were among the last to be settled in the West and among the first to be forsaken. Indeed, the entire process of homesteading and abandonment occurred in just twenty-two years, between 1908 and 1930. From the historian's point of view, this rapid succession of very different communities, each with its own economic imperatives, presents a rare opportunity to examine the relationship between culture and ecology within a reasonably well-defined area.

If we are ever to grasp the ecological transformation of the Canadian plains, we must focus on this succession of prairie cultures. As the historian William Cronon has said, "The replacement of Indians by predominantly European populations . . . was as much an ecological as a cultural revolution, and the human side of that revolution cannot be fully understood until it is embedded in the ecological one."[3] Each culture used and therefore modified the environment differently. Each modification, in turn, helped shape the opportunities available to the dominant culture of the time and to succeeding cultures. Only with knowledge of this reciprocal relationship can we appreciate the nature and scale of the environmental change that has occurred and some of the mechanisms behind it.

How much each culture changed the plains environment depended on its perception of the economic utility of the plains environment in its existing state. As long as non-natives could see little profit in what was to become southwestern Saskatchewan, they left most of it alone. During that period, lasting until about 1880, the area was central only to a way of life that enveloped both the Native Peoples and Métis of the larger plains ecosystem. To them, the grassland remained a source of plenty until buffalo became a commercial resource and the rate of harvesting buffalo exceeded the rate of natural replenishment. The ranchers who succeeded the Native Peoples and Métis as the dominant plains culture from 1880 to 1908 pursued a generally benign relationship with the environment until obliged by shifting government policies to fence the range, at which point they had to adopt more self-sustaining grazing methods or face the loss of pastures through environmental degradation caused by overstocking. Natives, Métis, and ranchers all produced their commodities within the existing natural order to a marked degree. External imperatives such as economic gain or legislation, however, made all three groups unconcerned until too late about the dominolike consequences of exceeding the regenerative capacity of the ecosystem.

Farmers differed from these three groups because they created an entirely new environment that had no inherent capacity to sustain itself. An offshoot of an agricultural system developed for a different environment, dryland farming did not work well as a means of production within the extremely dry south country and the ecology of monoculture cereal production required vigilant protection to survive in the area. In addition, the use of new farming technologies hastened environmental change until traces of the earlier buffalo landscape all but disappeared. This collision of natural and human forces, legislated into being by governments eager to attract settlers to the West, and sustained by science and technology, has led us to the environment we know today.

In this century agriculture and to a lesser degree urbanization have transformed more than 80 percent of Canada's native prairie landscape. By 1931, some 60 percent of southern Saskatchewan's grasslands were under cultivation. Today, 47 percent (66,386,074 acres or 26,886,359 ha) of Saskatchewan's total land base (140,878,080 acres or 57,055,622 ha) is used as farmland and 24 percent is productive cropland. Land left as summer fallow has increased from 7,275,000 acres (2,946,375 ha) in 1931 to 14,116,700 acres (5,717,263 ha) in 1991. Some 90 percent of the rough fescue grassland that greeted the first Euro-Canadians to explore the area in the mid-1850s has fallen before the plow, and grazing and haying practices have modified much of the rest. As a result, almost the entire tallgrass prairie is gone. Only one-fifth to one-quarter of the once-abundant short-grass prairie, the mixed grass prairie, and the aspen parkland remains in what we, too optimistically, call a native state.

Wildlife populations have been similarly devastated. To avoid starvation in the aftermath of the buffalo's destruction, the Native Peoples and Métis were reduced to depleting the stock of other indigenous animals. The ranchers took up arms against such perceived competitors as the wolf. Farm expansion removed nearly three-quarters of prairie wetlands, resulting in a sharp decline in waterfowl populations. In the past two hundred years, we have extirpated the swift fox, the black-footed ferret, the elk, the plains wolf, and the plains grizzly. There are no more free-ranging buffalo. Other species, such as the burrowing owl, hover on the brink of extinction. The status of many other prairie species is unknown.

One of the problems in detecting environmental change, even when its cumulative impact is so great, is the brevity of our personal experience. Although the changes over the course of the past century and a half have been drastic, individually we are hard-pressed to detect the impact of a single change. Only during a brief environmental catastrophe, or by studying cumulative change, do we become sensitive to ecological effects and their probable causes. Even then, we must rely on scientists to interpret the meaning of such changes. Historically, the matter becomes even murkier. Not only do we lack plentiful, reliable observations of local environmental change over time, we are largely unable to discern any baseline for the few observations that do come to light. Change may seem apparent, but change *from* what? That is the subject of this book, as it looks at the effects of three very different economic and cultural regimes on the environment of southwestern Saskatchewan.

THE BUFFALO
PLAINS

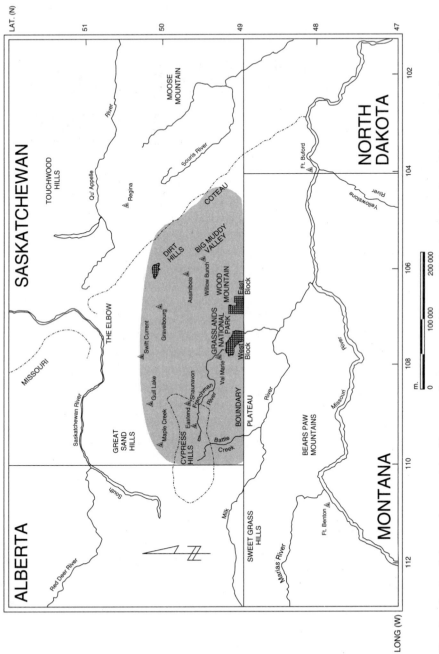

The Grasslands of the southern prairies. The approximate geographic area of the book is indicated by the shaded area. The boundaries of the Grasslands National Park are also approximate.

ONE
Buffalo As a Way of Life

Few non-natives visited southwestern Saskatchewan before 1850. Other than an occasional trapper or trader, Euro-Canadians had little interest in and even less knowledge of the area. The Great Plains were the domain of the Native Peoples who had tied their lives to the migrations of the buffalo for millennia. What little we know of the area in these times comes mainly from the reports of early traders, explorers such as John Palliser and Simon J. Dawson, officers of the North-West Mounted Police, members of the British North American and United States boundary commissions, and government-sponsored geologists and botanists who mapped the area before settlers arrived.

The Buffalo Landscape

During the warm weather of spring, summer, and early fall, large encampments dotted the grassy plains as the Native Peoples hunted buffalo and other foraging game. When the weather became inclement, the people divided into smaller groups and retreated with scattered herds of buffalo to the wooded uplands where shelter, water, and firewood were abundant for the winter months. They were what historian John S. Milloy has aptly called "buffalo people." Buffalo were central to their lives, governing their level of subsistence, affecting their relationships, and shaping their spiritual beliefs. The buffalo, in turn, depended almost wholly upon the naturally curing grasses of the vast plains that extended more than five thousand miles (8000 km) from north to south. As fared the buffalo, so fared the people: ecology, economy, and culture were one.

Despite evidence suggesting a near-absence of buffalo on the Great Plains between 5000 and 2500 B.C., and again from A.D. 500 to 1300, the herds clearly dominated the grassland region from the fifteenth century onward. Recent estimates place their number at around 28 to 30 million head for the Great Plains as a whole. While this is one-quarter to one-third of the previously accepted estimates of the total plains buffalo population, it is nonetheless a substantial figure, suggesting a density of nine to ten animals per square mile (3–4 animals/km²). As buffalo tend to migrate in large herds, great concentrations of the animals came to certain parts of southwestern Saskatchewan each year.

While he was near Moose Jaw Creek in 1858, Palliser recorded that "the whole region as far as the eye could reach was covered by buffalo, in bands varying from hundreds to thousands."[1] Similarly, Captain Anderson of the British North American Boundary Commission survey of 1873–74 observed: "The buffalo were met with here in great herds. . . . For about 100 miles [160 km] of longitude, the plain was swarming with countless herds of buf[f]alo, and, like an invasion of locusts, they swept everything before them."[2] His fellow surveyor L. F. Hewgill said that

> The picture of the Boundary Commission being "held up" by these animals for 24 hours will probably convey more to the reader who had never seen them than any other illustration I could give. . . . Lt. Greene of the U.S. Engineers, told the writer he had estimated a herd, by timing them passing a given point, that he was sure they were over three miles [5 km] long and that the herd contained from 75,000 to 100,000. . . . I have been told by half-breeds that they have seen the Saskatchewan River bridged by the carcasses of the drowned buffaloes, the ones in the rear having forced them on to the insecure ice till the river was blocked, and the living ones passed over on the bodies of their drowned friends.[3]

The possibility of exaggeration aside, there seems little doubt that buffalo heavily populated southwestern Saskatchewan seasonally until the final quarter of the nineteenth century.

Buffalo were such bulky beasts that they had a profound effect on the land as they passed through on their annual migrations. Wherever they marched in line over the semi-arid plains, they left virtual highways of hard-packed earth. As no vegetation grew on these trails, they became the sites of accelerated soil erosion. Speaking of the deep ravines of the Milk River area in 1873, Captain Featherstonhaugh, also of the Boundary Commission, said that "these contain narrow buffalo paths, along which the herds pass in search of water, or in order to cross to the north."[4] Buffalo archeologist George Arthur has written convincingly of "a vast network of well-worn trails, usually between the tablelands and watercourses."[5]

Buffalo are heavy grazers and when traveling in large herds rapidly denude the country through which they pass. Near Moose Jaw Creek, Palliser compared their effect to that of a plague of locusts, reporting that the huge herds had cropped the grass so short that "[I] began to have some serious apprehensions for my horses."[6] When the North-West Mounted Police trekked west in 1874, frequently holding to the Boundary Commission trail along the 49th parallel, they rarely found grass in recently grazed areas to be more than three inches (8 cm) high. Trampling was a further direct effect of the herds on vegetation, particularly when the animals crowded into small copses to escape the heat. In such circumstances, the underbrush might be all but eliminated. With the combined effect of rubbing against and uprooting trees this was, as Arthur has written, "doubtless an important factor in checking the invasion of prairie by aspen and other timber, and hence, was an integral element in the maintenance of grassland ecology."[7]

Buffalo also left their mark on the landscape through the creation of wallows: shallow pits, usually only about two feet (60 cm) deep, with a diameter of between ten and twenty feet (3–6 m). The wallows of a large herd might cover many acres, usually on level ground but sometimes on moderate slopes as well. There were both dry and wet wallows. We think that buffalo created dry wallows to help them shed their heavy winter coats, while the wet wallows were the result of attempts to escape biting insects or simply to keep cool. Wallowing also seems to have been more common during the rutting season. The visual effect on the landscape would have been not unlike a golf course with closely spaced sand traps; the ecological effect was one of spotty devegetation followed by accelerated erosion.

The herds gravitated to lakes, streams, and sloughs as they grazed. Historical reports show they trampled the moist ground adjacent to these bodies of water into a hummocky landscape and that they churned up and fouled the water itself. One observer described water holes as "mere mud trampled into paste."[8] The effect was so pronounced that horses sometimes refused to drink at such spots. To those travelers who closely followed the movements of antelope to find water in this dry country, arrival at a water hole often brought intense disappointment. Members of the Boundary Commission, for example, reported that

The buffalo find every pool of water existing upon the prairie, and are in the habit of standing in them to rid themselves of the flies which are their peculiar pests. Wherever, therefore, the buffalo had preceded us we found the pools were mud-holes, which were loaded with buffalo *excreta*. Sometimes the water which we were compelled to drink, even of pools large enough to be called ponds or small lakes, was so impregnated with buffalo-urine as to partake of its color, and to be altogether disgusting to the stomach.[9]

Despite this, many had no choice but to consume the water. North-West

Mounted Policeman J. E. McEntyre, traveling from Fort Walsh to Fort Benton in 1879, found that "water was at a premium and on two occasions I was forced to use water for tea or coffee obtained from a buffalo wallow, where these animals had been im[m]ersing themselves, but it was a case of do or die, either use what we could find or go without."[10] Obviously, the impact of the buffalo on bodies of water was substantial throughout this semi-arid country.

The passage of so many animals also left its impression on the land in the form of dried buffalo dung, more commonly called chips, which literally covered the prairies. As one student of the phenomenon phrased it, "'When the chips are down,' may well have been coined by the first person to see the evidence left in the wake of a passing bison herd."[11] Dry chips were almost the only means of making a fire for warmth or cooking in the treeless land between Wood Mountain and the Cypress Hills. While near Wood Mountain in 1874, George M. Dawson of the Boundary Commission became enthusiastic about the "abundance" of chips; one hundred miles (160 km) farther west he remarked, with perhaps less fervor, that his party was "wholly dependent" on them for fuel. Their practical utility aside, the chips have been described as "undoubtedly an important component in maintaining the grasslands of North America." It has also been argued, plausibly, that their ubiquity contributed significantly to the devastation of nineteenth-century prairie fires. To quote Dawson again, "Dry buffalo chips once taking fire could hardly be put out & often served to set the grass going [on fire] again."[12]

Without tens of millions of buffalo grazing far and wide for millennia, the Great Plains would have been a strikingly different place. In wet years the grasses themselves would have been much taller, not unlike the "stirrup-high" species that greeted the first farm settlers. The trees that the buffalo routinely trampled or reduced to splinters would have achieved more than a foothold in this semi-arid land. Without the ubiquitous wallows and hard-packed trails, the hillsides would have remained an uninterrupted carpet of grass. Both land and water would have been less fouled.

While buffalo affected the regional environment simply by virtue of their numbers and size, a host of other species also contributed to the presettlement landscape. Many early visitors to southwestern Saskatchewan commented on the pock-marked character of the prairies resulting from the abundance of badgers. Members of the Boundary Commission spoke of the innumerable badger-holes honeycombing the plains. Similarly, Robert Bell of the Geological Survey of Canada called badgers the "commonest" animal on the plains, and described the ground of southwestern Saskatchewan as "riddled" with their holes.

Prairie dogs, which may have been just as common in some parts of southwestern Saskatchewan, created a similar landscape. Unfortunately historical accounts of them are rare. Hewgill wrote only that "their villages contain many thousands . . . always in sandy soil." He noted further that their burrows provided a home to both rattlesnakes and burrowing owls. Likening their environmental effect to that of gophers, historical geographer J. G. Nelson has said that such burrowing creatures increased water absorption and retarded runoff to streams. They also counteracted the packing of soils caused by large mammals grazing on uncultivated rangelands. At the same time, they competed vigorously with grazing animals for vegetation. One early study of prairie dogs found that 32 prairie dogs consume as much grass as 1 sheep and 256 prairie dogs as much as 1 cow.

While prairie dogs and bison competed directly for grass, antelope, deer, and elk had different tastes, which helps to explain why all were originally found in such numbers in southwestern Saskatchewan. Antelope prefer the leaves of shrubs and forbs (herbs other than grass), whose growth is aided significantly by the moderate to heavy grazing associated with buffalo. This also explains the close association between antelope and prairie dog colonies, where forbs are the most common form of vegetation. Deer and elk, while exhibiting similar preferences, also browse on willow and aspen buds, particularly during the winter months. Not only did the eating habits of these animals complement one another, but the winter browsing of the deer and elk may have contributed significantly to the retardation of poplar growth, thereby helping to maintain the grasslands as an ecosystem.

Because buffalo, deer, elk, prairie dogs, and other creatures were so plentiful, many predators found the presettlement grasslands a congenial habitat. Wolves, coyotes, and swift foxes were particularly common, although grizzly bears also thrived amid such rich game resources. When fur trader Peter Fidler visited the Elbow of the South Saskatchewan River in 1800, for example, he saw ten grizzlies in just a few days. Half a century later, John Palliser said grizzlies were still abundant. As long as herbivores inhabited the southern Canadian plains in large numbers, predators of many species remained numerous as well.

Prairie Fire

The grasslands of southwestern Saskatchewan were, quite literally, ablaze each spring and fall during the presettlement era. Lightning was one important cause. Despite the primordial origins of lightning fires, scientists were until recently divided about the impact of lightning on the plains. Some went so far as to ascribe all fires to people. In 1956, for example, Omer C. Stewart claimed that his investigations had revealed no evidence that lightning caused plains fires. More recently, the work of E. V. Komarek and others has proven that lightning has always been a significant influence on the nature of the world's grasslands. Looking at western Canada as a whole in the presettlement era, J. G. Nelson and R. E. England concluded that historical references identified lightning as a common source of fire. With specific reference to southwestern Saskatchewan, J. S. Rowe has documented many grass fires originating from lightning strikes.

Native Peoples were the second major cause of grassland fires, although their role has not always received the attention it deserves. Sociologist Johan Goudsblom has said that the domestication of fire represented "the first great ecological transition brought about by humans."[13] Referring to North America, he described the plains and prairies as largely the result of the burning practices of Native hunters. Stephen Pyne, an authority on the history of fire in North America, calls fire-setting a cultural phenomenon, among humans' oldest tools, and he urges that it be considered an important component of environmental change. He states that "the evidence for aboriginal burning in nearly every landscape of North America is so conclusive, and the consequences of fire suppression so visible, that it seems fantastic that a debate about whether Indians used broadcast fire or not should ever have taken place."[14] Plant ecologist Don Gayton, referring to the western Canadian prairies, said that "man has always been a creature of grasslands and savannah, and his presence in North America is probably intimately linked to fires and the maintenance of grasslands."[15]

Although no historical observers of the western interior consciously set out to record the incidence of prairie fires, their cumulative testimony is unequivocal about both the frequency and seasonal timing of these conflagrations. Each year fires burned broad stretches of the plains. They commonly started in either spring or fall and required little encouragement to burn hundreds of square miles of territory. Statistically, April and October were the two months of the year in which fires most often occurred. Anderson of the Boundary Commission wrote that

The latter part of the autumn season [1874] had not passed without one or two incidents worthy of record. The heat of the sun and the excessive drought during the summer had completely parched the prairie-grass, and the soil was fissured in all directions. Although the greatest vigilance was practised, the occurrence of prairie-fires seemed inevitable, and towards the end of August a pillar of smoke visible to the north, a great distance off, gave warning that before many days were past, the whole of the Great Plains would be swept by fire. The course of the fire was most capricious, and often turned by a ravine, or by a slight change in the wind, into a new course. The onward progress of the fire was noticed for many days by the gradually-increasing temperature of the air, and soon by the smell of burning grass.[16]

Anderson's graphic account points indirectly to the inability of people to control such fires. George Dawson, commenting on the month of September in the same year, mentioned the probable carelessness of a pipe-smoker in setting the grass ablaze and said that his men were not able to extinguish the resulting blaze. Nature itself had few defenses against fire in the dry, open south country, although rivers, lakes, and sloughs; areas of sandy soil with little vegetation; and sharp upslopes restricted its spread to a limited extent. Only when rainfall was abundant throughout the growing season and the snows came early was the prairie free of fire.

Scholars have advanced many explanations for the motivations of the Native Peoples in firing the grass. Some early students of the topic adopted the view that early humans were congenital arsonists. Others of more balanced perspective have cited reasons including signaling, hiding the tracks of travois during warfare, and controlling wildlife movements. The latter reason is the one most commonly referred to in historical accounts. In 1859, for example, Simon Dawson noted that

> One object in burning the prairie . . . was to turn the buffalo; they had crossed the Saskatchewan in great numbers near the Elbow and were advancing toward us, and crossing the Qu'Appelle not far from the height of land; by burning the prairie east of their course, they would be diverted to the south, and feed for a time on the Grand Coteau, before they pursued their way to the Little Souris, in the country of the Sioux, south of the 49th parallel.[17]

In a similar vein, Hudson's Bay Company trader Isaac Cowie recorded that in mid-June of 1868 the northward migration of the buffalo across the Missouri had been "deflected" away from the hunting territories of the Native Peoples of the Qu'Appelle and the Touchwood Hills, and directed much farther west into the country of the Blackfoot and their allies. He was not certain of the cause, but suggested it was either fire or the deliberate action of the Missouri River Indians. One need not subscribe to Pyne's notion that Native Peoples used fire to "cultivate" the landscape to read instances like this as showing that they conceived of fire as a means of simplifying existence on the plains.

The frequency with which lightning strikes occurred, or for that matter the precise intent of the Native Peoples in setting fire to grassland, is of less importance here than the impact that recurrent burning had on the plains environment. As integral members of that ecosystem, wholly dependent on its food chain, the Native Peoples were directly affected. When the result was as it seems the Native Peoples intended, it made their lives much easier. Like Simon Dawson and others, Sam Steele of the Mounted Police said the Native Peoples set fires to encourage the return of the buffalo in the spring. Similarly Marcel Giraud, an authority on the plains Métis, stated that Native Peoples sometimes burned the grass to provide better pasturage for their horses.

Scientific research has proven that burning does indeed improve pasturage. Chemical analysis shows that the new grass that appears after burning is nutritionally better, as the volume of indigestible plant material is lower and the percentage of foods and minerals in new shoots higher. It may also be that grazing animals such as buffalo are attracted to areas of new grass because without plant litter they can easily graze the grass right down to the ground. At the same time, uncontrollable fires could just as easily destroy many buffalo, consume personal property, and, on occasion, kill people. It also inevitably reduced the buffalo chips in its path to ashes, making traveling in treeless country even more difficult than usual.

The effects of annual burning on other inhabitants of the plains were equally mixed. In the short term, of course, spring fires might be devastating to ground-nesting birds, or take a significant toll of newborn buffalo calves or young antelope. Creatures that used burrows, such as prairie dogs, badgers, burrowing owls, or rattlesnakes, would have been less affected. On the other hand, once the burned area had recovered, some species, such as the pronghorn antelope, would likely have found the tender new grass as much to their taste as did the buffalo, particularly during the spring and autumn. Prairie chickens, nesting waterfowl, and sandhill cranes have also been found to benefit significantly from the more vigorous plant growth that follows burning.

The effects of fire on regional vegetation are more difficult to assess. While scientists once vigorously debated the impact of recurrent fire on grasslands, most now agree that it aids in suppressing the growth of trees thereby helping greatly in the formation and maintenance of the grasslands. This happens because grass recovers much more quickly from burning than woody plants do. In fact, woody species that do not sprout from their roots may be eliminated, or at least be greatly thinned out, by burning. The impact on forbs, which are important to antelope and deer, is less clear, although it seems that in most grassland ecosystems around the world fire tends to favor their proliferation. Perennial grasses customarily sprout one to three weeks earlier than usual on burned areas and may remain green longer. This occurs because the denuded soil tends to be warmer during the daytime. At first glance, then, the attractiveness of such growth to grazers such as buffalo suggests that the Native practice of burning in the fall may have lured game to their territories. In the northern plains, however, the susceptibility of these early grass seedlings to spring frosts could easily offset this advantage. It could also be nullified over the longer term by buffalo eating the shoots down to the ground, thereby severely taxing the root reserves and jeopardizing the possibility of recovery. That the Native Peoples persisted in burning the grasslands year after year seems to indicate that they found the practice to their advantage more often than not.

Native Peoples

There were two main groups of Native Peoples who made their home in this area: the allied Assiniboine, Saulteaux (Ojibway), and Plains Cree, and the Blackfoot, Peigan, and Blood of the Blackfoot Confederacy. Later, they were joined by Sioux seeking sanctuary in Canada from the United States army. Certain locales around the border of the southwest were blessed with enough water to create excellent wildlife habitats. The interior lands, by contrast, were drier with fewer trees, making them less hospitable to game and people alike. The Native Peoples kept mostly to the borders of the dry interior, drawn to the fertile areas with their promises of water and abundant game.

To the east was Wood Mountain, or Woody Mountain as it was often called in the nineteenth century, with its streams and springs, sheltered coulees, and abundant trees. To the explorers, and no doubt to the Native Peoples as well, this was a veritable oasis on the edge of a desertlike wilderness. Travelers saw it as the final opportunity to stock up on kindling wood before setting out across the treeless plains. Although buffalo chips always fueled fires for cooking on the semi-arid prairies, it still took a few wood shavings and a bit of kindling to ignite the dried dung. As L. F. Hewgill of the British North American Boundary Commission recorded:

> "Buffalo chips" were collected at all the camps in large sacks, and made excellent fuel, even after a shower of rain the under part was always dry. Of course it was necessary to have a small supply of wood to start your fire, but once it was lit and fairly started there was no more trouble.[18]

Isaac Cowie, a young apprentice clerk with the Hudson's Bay Company, records the historical richness of the local game and fur resources. In 1868, he traded at his Wood Mountain post for "485 prime buffalo robes, 22 buffalo bosses, 79 buffalo tongues, 21 prime badgers, 1 grizzly bear, 21 red foxes, 132 kitt [swift] foxes, 16 hares (Jackrabbits), 3 skunks, 1 wolverine, [and] 59 wolves."[19] Between mid-century and at least the 1870s the Assiniboine dominated this area, although Cowie also mentions trading at

Wood Mountain in the Saulteaux (Ojibway) language. To the northwest, Old Wives Lake offered equal abundance. Cowie, visiting an outpost of Fort Qu'Appelle at Old Wives Lake in 1868, said the post's inventory comprised 90 buffalo robes, 70 buffalo tongues, 5 badgers, 5 red foxes, 20 kitt foxes, 1 lynx and 20 wolves. He also noted that "the ground seemed to be honeycombed with badger holes."[20] This northerly country, according to a map drawn by members of Palliser's expedition, was Cree territory.

Northwest of Wood Mountain, Palliser mapped the Elbow of the Saskatchewan as a crossing place suitable for wagons. The shallow ford at that great crook in the river near the Sand Hills was used not only by Native Peoples and the occasional explorer, but also by the great herds of buffalo that passed through the area each year. Palliser noted on his map, "On the Plains near the Elbow vast herds of Buffalo were met with, & in the valley abundance of Wapiti, Small Deer, & Grizzly Bears. In the River, Beaver are very common."[21] When the Dawson-Hind expedition crossed the plains in 1859, Simon Dawson also recorded seeing many buffalo near the Elbow. Fifteen years later, Bell said he, too, saw huge herds at the crossing on what he called "their annual migration."[22] Considering this sustained abundance, it is not surprising that on his maps Palliser showed the Elbow as flanked by many Blackfoot camps on the west and Cree camps on the east.

To the west, many streams drained the Cypress Hills giving rise to beaver colonies, but otherwise the game resources were similar to those at Wood Mountain. Cowie, who established a trading post at Cypress Hills in 1871, observed that

As far back as the memory and traditions of the Crees then living extended, these Cypress Hills . . . had been neutral ground between many different warring tribes, south of the now marked international boundary, as well as the Crees and Blackfeet and their friends. No Indian for hunting purposes ever set foot on the hills, whose wooded coulees and ravines became the undisturbed haunt of all kinds of game, and especially abounded in grizzly bears and the beautifully antlered and magnificent was-cay-sou, known variously by the English as red deer and elk.[23]

George Dawson heard a similar story about "neutral" territory more to the south and west of the Cypress Hills from W. G. Conrad, a trader familiar with both the American and Canadian plains. Captain Featherstonhaugh repeated the latter claim, adding that

The plains between Milk River and the Three Buttes are a sort of neutral ground between the Indian tribes, and are generally left unoccupied by them; the Sioux and the Assinebonies [sic] do not appear to cross to the west bank of the stream, and the Blackfeet, who cling to the skirts of the Rocky Mountains, rarely approach the Buttes.[24]

This interpretation of the Cypress Hills as a neutral ground has not gone undisputed. Archeologists Robson Bonnichsen and Stuart J. Baldwin have argued that far from being a no-man's land, the Cypress Hills were actually an "any man's land" whose natural abundance was well exploited by various Native Peoples. Both archeological evidence and the historical record suggest they are right.

According to Cowie, the Cypress Hills fell within Blackfoot territory. The allied Assiniboine, Cree, and Saulteaux visited the Hills at their risk, but visited nonetheless. He said that in 1868 a combined camp of Assiniboine, Cree, Saulteaux, and Métis ventured into the Sandy Hills some twenty miles (30 km) north of the Cypress Hills, which they recognized as Blackfoot territory.[25] This seems consistent with Palliser's 1858 observation that the Blood tribe (a member of the Blackfoot Confederacy) frequented the Cypress Hills. Palliser's maps also show a number of Blood encampments in the Sand Hills. We may take establishment of a Hudson's Bay Company wintering post on the east slope of the Cypress Hills in 1871 as further evidence of Native use of the area, especially in light of Cowie's admission that this post "at which the ever hostile Blackfeet and Qu'Appelle Indians [Cree, Assiniboine, and Saulteaux] would meet, was not at all desirable."[26]

In 1877, when Superintendent James A. Walsh of the North-West Mounted Police assembled the local Native Peoples at Fort Walsh to conduct a census, he found 47 lodges of Cree, 60 of Saulteaux, and 189 of Assiniboine. One hundred and forty-five lodges of the latter, in Walsh's words, "claim as their territory all the land from the west end of Cypress Hills to Wood Mountain, and from the Milk River to the South Saskatchewan."[27] Unquestionably this was disputed territory throughout the nineteenth century, but it seems equally clear that we should not take territorial disagreement to imply a lack of natural resource use.

To the south, the Sweet Grass Hills and the Bears Paw Mountains on the southern side of the 49th parallel were the American counterparts of the Cypress Hills. In 1872 the chief astronomer with the United States Boundary Commission reported that the Sweet Grass Hills are

The center of the feeding-ground of the great northern herd of buffaloes. This herd, which ranges from the Missouri River north to the Saskatchewan, made its appearance, going south, about the last of August. The number of animals is beyond all estimation. Looking at the front of the herd from an elevation of 1,800 feet above the plain, I was unable to see the end in either direction.[28]

Hewgill confirmed that from the Sweet Grass Hills to Chief Mountain buffalo were "innumerable." This, all agreed, was Blackfoot territory. Immediately east of this point, and especially along the Milk River, was the land explorers knew as the neutral zone.

Although various tribes hunted in and around southwestern Saskatchewan throughout the nineteenth century, it is difficult to arrive at any conclusions regarding the number of Native Peoples involved. The estimates provided by observers are too gross in scale and too infrequently made to be of much use. Historical geographer Arthur Ray, who tallied Palliser's count of Native Peoples, provided the following numbers for Plains Cree at specific points in 1863:

Moose Mountain	100 lodges
Moose Jaw	120 lodges
Couteau de Prairie	400 lodges [29]

Interpreting a lodge generously to be 6 people, this equals a Cree population of some 3720 on the eastern and northern edges of the area. No comparable figures are available for Assiniboine and Saulteaux, who appear to have hunted around Wood Mountain. Palliser said only that there were about 1000 Assiniboine in all of what is now the Province of Saskatchewan, and another 4000 between the international border and the Missouri River. Similarly, Palliser estimated the number of Blackfoot, Blood, and Peigan to be 600, 2800, and 4400, respectively. Superintendent Walsh's 1877 census of Indians encamped at Cypress Hills is more precise. Again assuming 6 people to a tent, the figures are 282 Cree, 360 Saulteaux, and 1134 Assiniboine. These figures are probably misleading, however, for the Indians were there specifically at Walsh's request and not necessarily because they frequented southwestern Saskatchewan.

Entirely absent from most accounts is any mention of Sioux, who had been coming into southwestern Saskatchewan from across the international boundary since at least the late 1860s. Cowie said, "They [the Sioux] had for years been spying out the land as one they wished to obtain possession of and therein to become good and loyal British Indians, supporting and trading with the Hudson's Bay Company."[30] In 1873 Hewgill saw a camp of some forty Sioux lodges on the Frenchman River. In the autumn of the same year, George Dawson reported thirteen lodges of Sioux at Wood Mountain. The North-West Mounted Police encountered a Sioux camp at Old Wives Lake in 1874. The demographic balance shifted again two years later when Sioux from the United States fled north into the Wood Mountain area to escape military retribution for their participation in the Battle of the Little Big Horn. Black Moon and fifty-two lodges of his followers came first, followed soon after by another fifty-seven lodges. By the end of the year, there were reportedly 500 men, 1000 women, 1400 children, and 3500 horses in the Sioux camp.

The Presettlement Balance of Nature

In the mid-nineteenth century, southwestern Saskatchewan was predominantly a land of grass, maintained by a semi-arid climate and annual fires. Reports of species using the south country are consistent enough to establish buffalo as the principal form of game, followed perhaps by antelope, deer, and elk. Predators such as coyotes, wolves, and grizzlies inhabited the area as well. Certainly the number of any species in any given year would have risen or fallen with weather patterns and resulting changes in vegetation and with Native harvesting patterns, yet no account fails to comment on the abundance and variety of fauna near the borderland oases. There is no doubt that buffalo dominated the ecosystem by virtue of their numbers and their physical bulk.

As many as seven different Native groups frequented this area until the 1870s. Typically, they used the oases on its borders more than they did its interior, which was poorer in natural resources and therefore less hospitable to people. As they had for millennia, the Native Peoples depended primarily on the herds of buffalo that ranged through southwestern Saskatchewan seasonally. The abiding abundance of animals suggests that Native populations did not exceed the natural carrying capacity of the land, and their semi-nomadic way of life, linked intimately to the seasonal availability of sustenance, helped to maintain this ecological balance.

At mid-century, humans and nature were more closely in balance in southwestern Saskatchewan than they would ever be again. As long as Native Peoples employed the natural resources of the plains according to traditional patterns of use, their age-old way of life remained intact and rewarding. Once they embraced a commercial view of their natural world, however, the decline of their culture became unavoidable.

TWO
Buffalo As a Commercial Resource

In 1690, when the Hudson's Bay Company sent Henry Kelsey inland from the coast to persuade the Natives of the plains to trade furs, the voluble young man from London found himself incapable of saying anything illuminating about his first sight of prairie grass. After crossing a narrow spit of grassland near the farthest northern extent of the Great Plains, Kelsey wrote in his distinctive Middle English verse that

> This plain affords nothing but Beast & grass
> And over it in three days time we past
> getting unto ye woods on the other side
> It being about forty six miles wide[1]

Intent on harvesting beaver and other fur-bearing animals, traders like Kelsey saw no utility in the plains. They were only too happy to leave the treeless grasslands behind and return to the fur-rich northern forests. Only the region's shallow, seasonal rivers held any appeal as they were the sole efficient means of transport between the fur fields and distant markets in London or St. Louis or New York. The situation was similar south of the 49th parallel. Few trappers and traders frequented the Great Plains region before 1830, and those who came did nothing to dispel the notion of an inhospitable land of limited economic opportunities. On those rare occasions when they committed their impressions to paper, it was only to suggest that the West was a hard land fraught with transportation problems, food shortages, and unpredictable Natives.

This view of the Great Plains persisted into the early nineteenth century. Meriwether Lewis and John Clark were the first to explore the upper Missouri watershed that drains southwestern Saskatchewan. Their 1804 quest for an all-water route across North America to facilitate continental trade and trade with the Far East was sponsored by Thomas Jefferson's administration. As most of their contemporaries considered the unknown lands between Atlantic and Pacific to be a curiosity at best and an obstacle at worst, Lewis and Clark's superb natural history data languished for lack of public interest in the resources they identified.

It was a party led by Major Stephen H. Long in 1819–20 that first planted a firm conception of the Great Plains in a broader segment of American society. Long led the scientific corps of a larger military expedition sent out by the United States government to check the westward advance represented by Lord Selkirk's British colony at Red River Settlement, near today's Winnipeg. Long reported that beyond the 96th meridian lay nothing but a "Great Desert," unfit for cultivation and therefore unsuited to settlement. Thus, to the extent that successive federal administrations and the American public at large had any distinct view of the land at mid-century, it was a negative one. The situation was no different north of the border. Unexplored and misunderstood by non-natives, the Great Plains remained a Sahara of the Euro-Canadian imagination.

The Trade in Buffalo Robes

Euro-Canadians and Americans may have considered the Great Plains an area to be traversed rather than exploited but the region did not completely escape the influence of British and American fur trading companies.

The Hudson's Bay Company, which dominated the entire trade of the North-West after amalgamation with the North West Company in 1821, had no commercial strength between the North Saskatchewan River and the 49th parallel. This was not for want of effort. The incursions of the American Fur Company and lesser commercial entities into the territory of the Blackfoot and other Native Peoples in the 1830s were noted with grave disapproval by the governor of the Hudson's Bay Company, George Simpson. His company responded with a series of brief trading forays into the south country. The most determined attempt was establishment of Bow Fort, also know as Peigan Post, on the Bow River near the gates of the Rockies, in 1832. This venture lasted only two years, after which distant Rocky Mountain House became the chief post for the Company's erratic and comparatively small Blackfoot trade.

Since about 1820, when big game became scarce near the growing Red River Settlement, Métis had visited the plains regularly to secure provisions for their own consumption and, increasingly, to trade. The Métis, people of mixed Native-white origin who had long been important in the fur trade of the western interior, made up most of Red River's population. During the early nineteenth century, their annual expeditions to the plains became the stuff of legends as they marched westward over the plains in paramilitary fashion, fearing no one, unrivalled in the efficiency with which they carried out their summer and fall hunts.

In the early years of the Métis buffalo hunt, its main purpose was the production of dried meat and pemmican for subsistence and for the provisioning of Hudson's Bay Company posts. In the 1830s, American traders, particularly those on the northern Great Plains, started to see buffalo robes as a substitute for declining beaver stocks, and Métis hunters began to hunt buffalo for their robes as well as for their meat. The trade grew considerably after the American fur markets reopened to the Métis at Pembina, just south of the 49th parallel, in 1844. The United States government supported this trade, astutely recognizing that a sharp decline in the great buffalo herds would ultimately repress Native culture more than the nation's military might. A succession of poor crops during the mid-1840s impelled ever more Métis to pursue the buffalo to earn a living, while the rising price of buffalo robes during the 1860s increased their participation in the trade even further. American competition obliged the Hudson's Bay Company, which initially had little but disdain for the robe trade, to compete.

In southwestern Saskatchewan, the Hudson's Bay Company did some minor trading with the Native Peoples through small wintering posts such as those at Wood Mountain, Cypress Hills, and Old Wives Lake. These posts, representing the weak southern advance of the company, were outposts of Fort Qu'Appelle, several hundred miles north on the Qu'Appelle River. There, from the late 1860s onward, Isaac Cowie traded in furs, pemmican, and buffalo robes mainly with the Assiniboine, Cree, and Saulteaux. Sioux sometimes attempted to trade at Fort Qu'Appelle as well, but Cowie actively discouraged this because of antagonism between the Sioux and his usual clientele.

More important than the trade carried out directly with the Native Peoples at the Hudson's Bay Company posts was the trade carried out through middlemen, many of whom were Métis or French-Canadians. Little is known about most of these independent traders, save for some of their names: George Fisher, James Francis, Antoine Hamelin, Joseph LaFournaise, Jean-Louis Légaré, Edward McKay, Antoine Ouellette, Frank Ouellette, Francis Whitford. Independent traders brought carts of Hudson's Bay Company goods both to large Native encampments and to Métis buffalo hunters. If a locality was frequented year after year, the trader might build a small log shanty such as that built on Mushroom Creek near today's community of Eastend. At other locations, where wood was even more scarce, the middlemen might build "mud houses" to accommodate their trade. Superintendent James Walsh of the North-West Mounted

Police recorded one of these on the Frenchman River in 1876. "The Mud House," he said, "was nothing more than a hole dug in the river bank and the front filled up with timber. It was used in winter by a half breed who came here from the north to trade with the Indians at this point."[2]

The volume of American trade with the Native Peoples and Métis of the northern plains was much greater than that of the Hudson's Bay Company. Occurring chiefly during the summer season at the time of the buffalo hunt, the American trade took place at a succession of posts on the upper Missouri River. After 1828 Fort Union, at the junction of the Missouri and the Yellowstone, was the entrepôt of the trade. The distillery that the American Fur Company operated there proved decisive in attracting the Native Peoples. Establishment of Fort McKenzie farther upstream provided the more westerly Blackfoot with better service after 1832. In 1846 Fort Benton, even farther upstream, supplanted McKenzie as the post of choice of the Blackfoot and Peigan in particular. During the late 1850s, the Bloods also traded at Benton.

As happened north of the 49th parallel, the American trading companies also worked through middlemen who staffed small outposts on the minor tributaries of the Missouri. Fort N. J. Turnay, an outpost built in 1872 and operated by one Francis A. Janneau, some twelve miles (20 km) up from the mouth of the Frenchman, drained its share of robes and furs from the Native Peoples of southwestern Saskatchewan, as did Wolf Point post, immediately east of Fort Peck. The trade in buffalo robes, and to a lesser extent tongues and hides, rose to a peak in the late 1860s to mid-1870s. In these years, the Métis became a force to be reckoned with on the plains.

The Métis and The Buffalo Hunt

Unlike the Native Peoples of the plains, whose patterns of consumption had enabled them to maintain a material culture based on buffalo for millennia, the Métis, with their increasing ties to the capitalist ethic that drove distant markets, were less concerned with subsistence than with profit. They began to view the buffalo principally as a commodity to be harvested for immediate gain. Once buffalo moved from being the mainstay of a subsistence economy to being a commodity subject to external market forces, the entire species was imperiled.

The Métis conducted two main buffalo hunts each year, one in early June and the other before freeze-up in the fall. There were many other less important hunts, but most lacked the intricate organization of the large summer and fall excursions onto the plains. The main summer hunt began in June and ended around mid-August. Upwards of one thousand Red River carts would start for the buffalo plains to the west of the Red River Settlement under a strictly enforced paramilitary structure. The slaughter lasted until the carts, which held some five hundred to one thousand pounds (230–450 kg) each, were full. Then the cavalcade turned back toward Red River, where traders eagerly awaited their return. After some three weeks in the settlement, perhaps one-third of the hunters would leave for the plains again, this time to return with fresh meat that would be frozen and eaten over the winter months.

The hunt's paramilitary organization was a defensive response to the hostility of the Native Peoples of the plains toward these annual Métis incursions. The historical record contains many references to Native displeasure at the activities of the Métis. Louis Shambow, for example, recalled going north into the Frenchman (Whitemud) River country in 1865 with a cavalcade of 250 to 300 carts and being stopped by a party of Assiniboine who said the Métis would advance farther north at risk of their lives. Ben Kline recalled an incident that took place in the 1860s, when smallpox had broken out among the northern Native Peoples:

> An epidemic of small-pox broke out among the Indians, who had a camp close to these [Métis] cabins. Fortunately, the newly-arrived half-breed hunters remained immune. This fact aroused the anger and jealousy of the Indians, who were losing many [of] their sick, especially the children. They maliciously visited the half-breed hunters camp, and did everything in their power to communicate the disease to them, without success, however.[3]

Cowie spoke for many observers when he said that "every one of the Indians resented the intrusion of the half-breed whites on the plains for hunting purposes."[4] As a result, they frequently attempted to disrupt the hunt, sometimes through intimidation, sometimes by trying to "deflect" the buffalo from their established grazing patterns, and sometimes by means of warfare. The latter reached a climax in 1851, when a small band of Red River Métis prevailed in a pitched battle with several hundred Sioux at the Grand Coteau southeast of what is now Minot, North Dakota. Afterwards the Métis were grudgingly respected as masters of the plains.

As far as we know, the Métis who hunted buffalo on the plains from about 1830 to 1880 did not set fires in an attempt to influence grazing patterns. The organization of their annual hunt was based on the principle of mobility, and this enabled them to go with relative ease to any region where large herds of buffalo were grazing. While the Native Peoples were also mobile, the Métis were utterly uninhibited by the territorial boundaries to which the Native Peoples subscribed.

The Native view of the Métis as formidable adversaries helps explain the impunity with which the Métis routinely took up winter residence in southwestern Saskatchewan. *Hivernement* (wintering) communities, as such congregations were known, accommodated Métis who had little wish to earn any of their living by farming. While many of their compatriots from the hunt took up residence on their river lots at Red River for the winter months, the *hivernants* (winterers) remained on the plains. *Hivernants* were at Wood Mountain and at Seventy Mile Crossing (later Val Marie) on the Whitemud or Frenchman River (*La Rivière Blanche*) by the late 1860s. Establishment of a permanent Métis settlement followed the rebellion at Red River Settlement in 1869–70, after which many Métis moved west. If they needed additional impetus, they found it in the fact that the buffalo herds were by that time customarily grazing so far west of the settlement that the Métis could no longer participate in the robe trade at all unless they wintered on the plains.

Métis Settlements

If proximity to the herds was the first criterion for selection of a permanent settlement, then proximity to fresh water and a supply of wood were considerations of the second and third order. The great authority on the plains Métis, Marcel Giraud, described the character of the typical location chosen by the buffalo hunters:

> The Métis scattered their huts in copses and in the wooded corridors that bordered the riverbeds, at the foot of the hills, or in the ravines that broke their slopes and which provided them, apart from wood, with the materials needed to construct hearths and chimneys, and, finally, in the coulees of the prairie—in fact anywhere that the bison went in search of shelter against snowstorms or of more easily accessible grass.[5]

Besides wood, water, and shelter, these sites customarily offered sloughs where hay was harvested in late summer as feed for cattle and horses and where a variety of fur-bearing mammals could be trapped for extra income during the winter. Permanent Métis communities such as the one at Wood Mountain also developed at Turtle Mountain, Moose Mountain, Fort Qu'Appelle, Cypress Hills, and at points farther north and west.

It is difficult for us to determine the impact that a Métis community such as the one at Wood Mountain would have had on the environment of southwestern Saskatchewan. It would have depended most on the size of the community. In 1870, thirty to forty families are said to have moved to Wood Mountain from the parishes of St. François-Xavier and St.-Joseph de Pembina under the leadership of George Fisher, a Métis trader. When Father Lestanc of the Roman Catholic Church arrived at the settlement in September of that year, however, he found about sixty families in residence. He also commented that another forty families lived three days farther west; presumably this was the settlement at Seventy Mile Crossing on the Frenchman River.

During the winter of 1871–72—an excellent one on the plains by all accounts—some 175 families settled at Wood Mountain. Captain Anderson of the British North American Boundary Commission counted some 80 families in 1872. In mid-August of 1873, Dr. Thomas Millman reported a community of 100 Métis families. In June of the next year George Dawson noted that all half-breeds of the region, which he placed at 100 to 200 families, were camping north of the Cypress Hills. With more apparent precision, Captain Anderson placed the 1874 population of Wood Mountain at 80 families. Even as late as 1877, with the buffalo herds dwindling markedly, there were reportedly about 150 families at Wood Mountain. These were extended families comprising not just immediate relatives but those related by marriage as well. Having weighed the evidence for the Métis community of Buffalo Lake in the same era, historians Beal, Foster, and Zuk have placed the average family size at ten people. On this basis, and taking 100 families to be more or less the usual size of the settlement, we can estimate the Wood Mountain population at around one thousand people throughout the 1870s.

This was a large community. It would have exceeded all in southwestern Saskatchewan except for the railway towns that were to come three decades later. Using logs for their dwellings, cooking, and heat, one thousand people would have had an impact on the timber resources of Wood Mountain. Yet when George Dawson came through in 1874, he recorded only that Wood Mountain Creek was "pretty well wooded along its banks with fair sized poplar."[6] The first indications of a wood shortage at Wood Mountain did not come until later.

The oxen that pulled the Métis carts, and the horses that they rode, would also have consumed a great deal of grass in a year. Unfortunately, we have no livestock numbers for the settlement. It is recorded that in 1873—an exceptional year for buffalo—a brigade of nine thousand carts under the direction of Gabriel Dumont left Wood Mountain to hunt farther west. If each cart were pulled by only one ox and not two, as often happened, the total is still high enough to have had a significant localized impact on the grass. Yet when the Mounted Police stopped at Wood Mountain in the spring of 1874, they had no difficulty purchasing seven tons (6.35 tonnes) of surplus hay for their horses. More than this, we simply do not know. The fact that the Métis returned to the Wood Mountain area year after year before settling there permanently suggests, however, that they placed little obvious strain on local resources.

The large cart brigades of the Métis hunters and freighters left a network of trails across the land. One trail used often by freighters extended diagonally across the eastern part of southwestern Saskatchewan, beginning at Fort Garry on the east, extending to Fort Ellice, and then cutting southwesterly through Wood Mountain to Forts N. J. Turnay and Peck on the American frontier. This was usually called the "traders road." We can trace another common avenue of Métis commerce from the border community of Pembina on the Red River in Manitoba to Turtle Mountain and on to Wood Mountain. Western extensions of these trails took the hunters to other Métis settlements on the Frenchman and Milk rivers and in the Cypress Hills. They could follow yet another trail, the "plains hunters trail," from Fort Qu'Appelle to the Cypress Hills. There were more direct north-south routes as well. These led from Métis settlements on the North Saskatchewan River to American posts on the Missouri. The wagons of the British North American Boundary Commission created the last major trail laid down along the 49th parallel in 1873–74. The North-West Mounted Police followed this trail at times during their 1874 trek across the plains, but otherwise it remained virtually unused, for, far from being a trail of commerce that connected trading centers, it led west solely out of political necessity.

The Decline of the Buffalo

Although southwestern Saskatchewan retained its presettlement environment much longer than other parts of the Canadian Great Plains, the days of the buffalo plains were numbered. To those living in or passing through a community that depended heavily on the buffalo as a resource, the annual harvest was always an important topic of discussion. Thus, we find Thomas Millman commenting on the abundance of buffalo at Wood Mountain in 1872 and Robert Bell expressing his amazement at their numbers just to the west two years later.

Within this cycle of abundance, there was occasionally a year of scarcity. The winter of 1870–71 was particularly bad. As Father Lestanc lamented, "Le buffalo était loin et en petit nombre/*Buffalo were few and far between*."[7] Although they returned in the next year, their course was ever more westward. According to local historian George Sheperd, after 1873 the herds never came back to the Wood Mountain district in large numbers. In 1875–76, only straggling herds were to be found east of the Cypress Hills, which caused the Métis to temporarily abandon the Wood Mountain community. What had happened? Under relentless pressure from

Native Peoples, Métis, and whites on both sides of the international boundary, the buffalo suffered an irreversible decline.

Estimates of the volume of the robe trade are scarce. In 1874, the well-traveled Reverend George McDougall had given the Department of the Interior a candid opinion about conditions in the North-West from Edmonton to Fort Benton on the Missouri. "I carefully observed the conditions of the natives," he wrote, "and the impression received was that an unmitigated wrong is being inflicted on a helpless wretched people."[8] He was referring specifically to the rise in liquor traffic across the 49th parallel, but even in the morally outraged minister's mind the deeper concern was the burgeoning trade in buffalo robes for which American traders paid with whiskey. McDougall estimated that in the spring of 1873 fifty thousand robes and pelts had been traded for liquor at Fort Benton. Historians Beal, Foster, and Zuk have noted, "The whiskey trade was actually the robe trade, liquor being merely the device and robes the object. . . . And the robe trade was the fundamental factor in the destruction of the great northern buffalo herds."[9]

During the 1830s one American Fur Company partner stated that his firm marketed 70,000 robes per year, that the Hudson's Bay Company sold 10,000 per year, and that other interests handled a further 10,000 robes annually. Another source, referring only to the American Fur Company, estimated a volume of 45,000 robes in 1839, 67,000 in 1840, and 110,000 in 1847. They harvested in the Missouri River watershed and shipped most of these robes to eastern markets via the Missouri. Fort Benton, the head of navigation on the Missouri, saw more than 400,000 robes pass over its docks between 1833 and 1858. They shipped an additional 760,000 robes downriver between 1859 and 1884. During more or less the same period, Hudson's Bay Company purchases are said to have averaged 10,000 robes per year, for a total of about another half million, although historian John Milloy suggests that the totals for the Hudson's Bay Company rose from an annual count of 200 in 1821 to 12,500 per year by 1842 and, after a small drop in 1849, to a high of 15,500 robes in 1860. Milloy also says that the Missouri River traders received "ten times the HBC totals."[10] Most of the robes harvested north of the 49th parallel were purchased from the Métis at either Fort Benton or Fort Garry (Winnipeg). Traders also obtained smaller quantities at posts such as Fort Qu'Appelle and its southern wintering posts at Wood Mountain and Cypress Hills. We will probably never know to what extent the demise of the buffalo was due to the robe trade, how much was caused by the American policy of starving the Native Peoples into submission, and how much was brought about by the delight sport hunters took in shooting the great beasts. Suffice it to say that by 1879–80, there were almost no buffalo left on the Great Plains.

A similar destruction was wrought on the wolves that had been abundant on the plains for most of the nineteenth century. They followed the enormous buffalo herds in packs and easily took down an aged or wounded animal or a newborn calf. They also feasted on the carrion left by the buffalo hunters. The latter predilection resulted in the deaths of tens of thousands. Wolfers would "salt" a carcass with strychnine, wait a day or two, and then return to skin as many as a hundred wolves at a time. In the 1870s the skins were worth from one to three dollars. Although this way of life earned wolfers the opprobrium of many—including the Native Peoples, who lost many dogs to the poison—it was among the easiest forms of profit-taking on the plains. As a result, they annually shipped thirty thousand wolf skins out of Fort Benton alone between 1875 and 1877. The result, as Campbell and Twining pointed out in 1878, was the almost complete absence of wolves on the plains.

Although the Canadian government did not act specifically to preserve the remaining game (and it is difficult to imagine how it could have enforced such legislation in any event), officials were aware that a shortage of food was a chief problem confronting the plains people. In 1876, E. A. Meredith, deputy minister of the interior, prepared a lengthy memorandum on what he called "The Food Question." Referring specifically to the buffalo, Meredith wrote that

> Some few years ago this supply of food seemed practically inexhaustible. But owing to the increase in White and Half-Breed hunters the Buffaloes have during the last few years been rapidly diminishing in numbers and there seems every reason to expect that under the existing state of things they will within the next decade of years, be entirely exterminated. To the Indians extermination of the Buffaloes means starvation and death.[11]

While Meredith was not convinced anything could be done to prevent eventual extirpation of the buffalo, he was certain their demise could be slowed if the robe trade were curtailed. Others, such as Indian Commissioner David Laird, agreed and argued for the imposition of export duties on robes and pemmican, and for prohibition of all buffalo hunting by whites and Métis during the winter and spring to prevent the slaughter of pregnant cows. Nothing came of these recommendations.

By 1879 the local food situation was so serious that all but a few Métis families had left Wood Mountain for good. Father Clovis Rondeau said that the buffalo were so far away that the Métis had no choice but to relocate or starve. Some five hundred people from Wood Mountain, Cypress Hills, and from the distant northern community of Batoche crossed into American territory to hunt along the Milk River.

This time, however, there could be no misunderstanding about the elimination of the herds. The buffalo were gone from southwestern Saskatchewan, as they were from the Great Plains region as a whole, and in their absence its ecology began to change markedly.

Buffalo Bones

While the best-known result of the destruction of the country's game resources is the signing of treaties by the Native Peoples of the plains during the 1870s, a less-studied result was their participation, with many Métis, in the new business of harvesting buffalo bones. In ecological terms, this harvest caused the final deliberate setting of prairie fires by the Native Peoples and eradicated the last signs of the true buffalo landscape.

The loss of the buffalo induced rapid, pronounced, and decisive change in Native and Métis communities. Already weakened by a smallpox epidemic in 1864–65 and another that broke out in 1869–70, the Cree, Assiniboine, and Blackfoot populations were in decline. The Cree, suffering less than most, took advantage of their numerical superiority to continue a concerted push to the west in search of the retreating herds. For a time they prevailed, but their defeat in battle at the hands of a group of Bloods and Peigans on the Belly (Oldman) River (near present-day Lethbridge) marked the end of their westward expansion. After that, the Cree and the Blackfoot and their respective allies hunted the dwindling stocks of buffalo and other game over shared territory. Without question, the Canadian Native People's perception of the plains as a place of declining resources was also influenced by the arrival of as many as five thousand Sioux from the United States in 1876. Certainly the Assiniboine saw it that way: in 1877 Superintendent James Walsh of the North-West Mounted Police reported that the Cree had refused to travel more than forty miles (65 km) east of the Cypress Hills owing to the presence of the Sioux. Because of this pragmatic realignment of territorial imperatives, the decision of nearly all Indian bands of the southern plains to take treaty is not surprising.

Métis, too, felt obliged to relocate to survive in a land of increasingly limited resources. Replacement of the Hudson's Bay Company trading post at Wood Mountain by another at Cypress Hills in 1871 was one indication of this shift, as was the deliberate division of the Métis community into the Wood Mountain and Milk River (on the American side of the line) settlements in 1872. From what we know of the demography of the Wood Mountain settlement in the 1870s, the size of the community remained fairly stable after this split: the Métis clearly recognized the carrying capacity of the local resource base.

The influx of Sioux into this territory, however, upset the Métis calculation drastically. Accounts throughout the late 1860s and 1870s place Sioux bands near most, if not all, of the Métis *hivernement* settlements on the plains. In a time of abundant game the presence of an additional few hundred people at each location probably meant little to the quality of Métis life, but once the buffalo herds diminished beyond all belief the impact of the Sioux was felt sharply. It is this that explains the 1874 petition from the Métis of the Qu'Appelle district to the Lieutenant-Governor of the North-West Territories seeking, among other rights,

> The right of hunting freely in the prairies west and southwest of the lakes Qu'Appelle without being arbitrarily hindered by the Indians but only in virtue of the regulations that the Indians, in concert with the Half-Breeds and the Government, shall establish hereafter for the good of all.[12]

The Métis who signed the petition were careful to point out that they had no intention of depriving the Native Peoples of their rights, but only wished to be able to live amicably with them and to encourage rational resource use. That the once all-powerful Métis *hivernants* would seek an agreement on hunting regulations said much about the newfound precariousness of life and the shifting balance of authority on the plains during the 1870s.

The government would not enact legislation of the kind sought by the Qu'Appelle Métis until 1894. By then, however, all the game resources of the southern plains, and not just the buffalo, were depleted. During their 1874 summer trek across the plains, the North-West Mounted Police had reported no game, "excepting ducks and prairie chickens," between Dufferin on the Red River and the Cypress Hills. As the summer of 1874 was exceptionally dry and marked by great prairie fires, it might be wrong to make too much of the police observations, but theirs was far from an isolated report. In 1879 J. E. McEntyre, a Mounted Police officer familiar with the south country on both sides of the line, confirmed the lack of game. Touring Indian Commissioner Edgar Dewdney observed that "the country south [of the South Saskatchewan River] is entirely destitute of game (that is, of small game)."[13] Jean L'Heureux, working for the government as a plains guide that year, noted in December the unusual sight of American soldiers giving rations to Canadian Blackfoot on the Elk River to prevent them from starving. The Native Peoples and the Métis were running out of alternatives.

Drawn west by the declining herds, and south by the American trading posts on the Missouri, the Native Peoples of the plains who had traditionally frequented southwestern Saskatchewan increasingly camped and hunted in the United States. While the distinction between Canadian and American soil meant little to most Native Peoples, government authorities saw matters differently. By 1877 so many Canadian Cree were crossing into the United States in search of relief that the American government established Fort Assiniboine partly to control transborder movement. This capricious "immigration," as some in government saw it, with the poor state of relations between the American government and its Native Peoples, led many Canadian officials to fear an international incident involving Canadian Native Peoples.

In 1880, four years after the Canadian government had effectively granted the Sioux sanctuary, Elliott T. Galt, the son of Canada's former high commissioner to Great Britain, traveled to Helena, Montana, to discuss ways of ensuring that Native Peoples who had signed treaty north of the border returned to Canadian territory. The Americans told Galt that members of the Blood, Blackfoot, and Cree tribes who were scattered between the Bears Paw Mountains and the foothills of the Rockies had little to eat. Equally destitute Sioux roamed the same territory. General Rugher, with whom Galt conferred, said that the Native Peoples had "very few buffalo left in that part of the country, nor clothing. He says that up to the present time they have behaved themselves very well yet he fears they may commit some indiscretion in which case they would have to be driven back by force."[14]

Left with little else, Native Peoples and Métis turned to the harvesting of all they had left of the once-abundant buffalo. Traditionally, the bones of the buffalo were among the most abundant and least desirable parts of the great beasts that resulted from the hunt. That is not to say, however, that bones were without their uses. The archeological record is clear on the utility of bones as tools and, to a lesser extent, as weapons and ornaments. We also know that Native Peoples often burned the bones to extract what George Dawson called their "fat," or marrow, for use in making pemmican. When this practice ended, at some indefinite point late in the nineteenth century, the prairie air was no longer "heavy with [the] smell and much ash."[15]

For the most part, however, the bones had been left on the open plains to bleach under the intense summer sun. To cite Dawson again, there were many parts of the plains, including the Coteau, that were littered thickly with the bones of recent hunts. Captain Anderson remarked that "in many places the bleached skulls and bones of the buffalo are scattered about, in evidence of the vast numbers that must formerly have grazed over the ground, and of the wholesale slaughter that has practically exterminated them in this section of country."[16] Indeed, the very name "Pile of Bones Creek," which was in common use at mid-century to refer to today's

Wascana Creek near Regina, suggests the size of the resource.

There was practically no market for bones from the plains before 1873. Demand grew when fertilizer producers and sugar refiners in the American Midwest, who used the phosphate from the bones in their processing, had exhausted the eastern and southern American bone supply. Their demand could not be satisfied, however, until the transportation network of the northern Great Plains improved. It was simply too expensive to collect bones by the cartload and then ship them on steamboats out of Fort Benton and other points on the Missouri. Construction of the Canadian Pacific Railway across the prairies in 1881 brought down freight costs and ensured that at least some indigent inhabitants of the region could earn a living. Jean-Louis Légaré, a French-Canadian trader based at Wood Mountain, bought more than 33,000 tons (30,000 tonnes) of bones locally for between $6 and $6.50 per ton between 1882 and 1888. Sioux who frequented the country between Wood Mountain and Moose Jaw also picked bones for a living.

Freight costs on the American side of the line decreased after 1883, when the Utah and Northern Pacific Railroad extended across Montana via the Yellowstone Valley. Farther north, the trading post at Wolf Point became the main collection point for bones harvested in carts by local Native Peoples and Métis, who received $4 to $4.50 a ton for their efforts. Without doubt, some Native Peoples who had routinely hunted in southwestern Saskatchewan were participants in this American market as well. Construction of the Great Northern "Hi-Line" immediately south of the 49th parallel took place during 1887 and the economies of station stops such as Malta, Montana, which would later become an important cattle shipping point, took root in the commerce of the bone trade.

With the buffalo gone, the grass grew thicker and higher until it was hard to find the bones. It then became common for the bone pickers to start fires that would make the bleached bones stand out clearly against the blackened prairie. These fires were small, as the pickers knew full well that too hot a blaze would consume their entire harvest. The setting of prairie fires, a vital part of the plains inhabitants' traditional cultural baggage, was given new, although brief, purpose by the demand of the $40 million trade in bones. In less than a decade the Great Plains of both Canada and the United States were picked clean.

Through Non-Native Eyes

The arrival of the railway—and the findings of the survey parties and scientific expeditions that had supplied the knowledge required for its construction—produced a marked change in the way non-natives viewed the

West. Equally able to cross the plains in a cost-effective straight line or to snake its way into the ore-rich foothills of the Rockies, the railway liberated investors, opening isolated areas and enlarging the potential scope and success of their investments. The railway was not, however, merely a means of facilitating private investment in the frontier; it was also a means by which governments applied their policies. North and south of the 49th parallel, business and government worked hand-in-hand to open the Great Plains to settlement. Capitalist logic, underpinned by government policy, created greater understanding of the region's economic utility. In the process, investors reaped profits and governments consolidated their sovereignty over vast territories. The geographically restrictive water-borne transportation and the lumbering ox carts of the Métis freighters was being replaced by the emancipating technology of the railway.

At the same time as buffalo robes were becoming increasingly important items of trade, exploring parties were at work charting the West for possible railway routes. The first to include any part of southwestern Saskatchewan in its purview was Isaac Stevens's 1853 search for a railway route between Minnesota and the northwest coast of the Pacific. Members of the Stevens party explored the upper tributaries of the Missouri before striking out across the plains to the Bears Paw Mountains, the Cypress Hills, and the Sweet Grass Hills. The land between the Missouri and the Milk rivers impressed them. Alert to the future of commercial rail traffic, Stevens characterized this as "an exceedingly fine grazing country."[17] He was less sanguine about the land north of the Bears Paw Mountains, next to the Milk River valley. On the advice of his colleague Tinkham, who explored that country, Stevens reported that

> Water is rarely found, and then only in some hole sheltered by the overhanging bank. All these things, with the almost total absence of animal life, the whistling, drifting sand of the dry river bed, gave rise to this portion of the Milk river valley, in the chilliness of autumn, the character of desolation and dreariness.[18]

Tinkham's findings quashed the limited interest that Stevens and his party had in exploring the country farther north.

North of the 49th parallel, Canadian nationalists, allied with the large manufacturing interests of Quebec and Ontario, saw the approaching end of Hudson's Bay Company rule in 1859 as an opportunity to press their claims to the western interior. Suddenly, this forsaken land seemed to capture everyone's attention. As a result, during the late 1850s two separate government-sponsored parties came west to investigate the character of the North-West. They were expected to determine the region's material resources, its climate, and its potential for construction of a railway wholly within British territory.

John Palliser led the first expedition. The heir to landed wealth in Ireland, Palliser first saw similar country during an 1847–48 hunting trip to the upper reaches of the Missouri River when he was just thirty years old. His popular book about those adventures made his public reputation and helped convince the Royal Geographical Society and the British government to underwrite his leadership of the first purely scientific expedition to British North America's western interior. Between 1857 and 1860 Palliser and his party explored from the Red River Settlement to the Pacific coast, and from the North Saskatchewan River to the 49th parallel. Their stout report and maps were a cornucopia of astronomical, meteorological, magnetic, and geological fact that provided the first reliable assessment of the interior's economic potential. These data offer us a rare glimpse of the mid-nineteenth century environment.

About a month and a half after Palliser launched his expedition, a second scientific party ventured into the western interior. Simon J. Dawson, a civil engineer best known for his survey and construction of the "Dawson Route" that connected Ontario with western Canada before the building of the Canadian Pacific Railway, led the expedition jointly with Henry Youle Hind, professor of chemistry at Trinity College in Toronto. Sponsored by the Canadian government, their expedition traversed only the area from Red River to the parklands and southern plains of what is now Manitoba and Saskatchewan.

The findings of the two parties of scientists were remarkably similar. Basically, their voluminous data divided the western interior into two zones of economic potential. Palliser characterized the first zone as a "fertile belt" that arched over the region from the Red River Settlement to the foothills of the Rockies in a trajectory that loosely followed the North Saskatchewan River. South of that great arc, occupying a much smaller triangular tract, were "arid plains," whose dry climate, sandy soil, and extensive grass cover proclaimed a future based on cattle grazing—Palliser's famous triangle.

Unnoticed by most readers of the Palliser and Dawson-Hind reports was a much smaller area within Palliser's arid plains, one butting up against the international boundary and extending from Wood Mountain to the Cypress Hills. Essentially, the tract took in today's southwestern Saskatchewan. Neither party explored it at all. Their only references to it—all of which were secondhand—identified it as the northern extension of the Great American Desert. That they dismissed it, both in their reports and on

their maps, as having no agricultural potential, ensured that it would remain a *terra incognita* to non-natives for many more years.

Both expeditions had selected their routes largely from existing Hudson's Bay Company reports and related maps that pertained to the flanks
of the major waterways with which fur traders were familiar. As many fur
trade posts had grown gardens successfully for decades, the arable character of this land was not in doubt. Palliser and Dawson-Hind therefore chose
to spend much of their time traveling across the unknown lands south of
the North Saskatchewan River, which had always generally defined the
southern limit of the company's trade.

During the 1850s there was much trouble between the Sioux and settlers immediately south of the international boundary. Recognizing that
Palliser's party might be in danger, his British sponsors warned him to
exercise the greatest caution in selecting a route. Specifically, the secretary of state for the colonies told Palliser he should avoid all risk of hostile
encounters. Dawson received similar advice. Palliser, who knew something of the American Natives because of his Missouri sojourn, ignored
the warning and headed straight south of Fort Garry, determined the location of the poorly marked international boundary, and followed it west. He
and his party eventually made their way to Moose Mountain before head-
ing north to Fort Ellice and then to Fort Qu'Appelle. From there Palliser
wished to go to the forks of the Red Deer River via the Elbow of the South
Saskatchewan. As Palliser contemplated the journey from the vantage point
of Fort Qu'Appelle, reestablished by the Hudson's Bay Company just two
years earlier, he observed that "westward of this . . . is unknown, and the
whole country in this latitude is untravelled by the white man."[19]

Palliser's conquest of this cartographic wilderness was, in fact, extremely
unadventurous. Occasionally, while in the company of Métis guides, he
and his men darted out onto the plains to the south, actually reaching Moose
Jaw and Thunder creeks once. Another time, they followed the South Saskatchewan west and then turned south to explore the Cypress Hills. They
then retreated to the distant north and west, where they spent most of the
next two years, knowing full well from their calculations that they had
skipped some four hundred miles (650 km) of territory immediately north
of the 49th parallel, the land extending from Moose Mountain to the Cypress Hills. When it came to identifying this country on the map that would
make him famous, Palliser had no alternative but to leave the entire section blank.

Dawson and Hind also concentrated their efforts on the valleys of the
Red and Saskatchewan rivers. Like Palliser, they moved south from Fort
Garry, followed the 49th parallel to the valley of the Souris, and then headed
north to Fort Ellice, whence they would follow Palliser's arc through Fort

Qu'Appelle and along the South Saskatchewan to the sand hills north of the Cypress Hills. Without having set much more than a foot on the short-grass plains to the south—"the great buffalo plains," as they called this country on one of their maps—they characterized it as unsuitable for agricultural settlement. But, as Hind's biographer has said, the explorer's conclusion, however correct, was "a broad perception . . . not a scientific insight."[20]

When the work of the Palliser and Dawson-Hind expeditions was done, no one would ever again view the North-West as a mere hinterland of the fur trade. Instead, as one historian has stated, "travellers [to the North-West] after 1857 began with the assumption not of an economy based on the wilderness but of the potential of an economy based on agriculture."[21] That is, with the exception of southwestern Saskatchewan, which remained unexplored but which both expeditions implied was an arid and inhospitable land.

Why did neither party explore the unknown south country? The answer is not entirely clear. They shared some fear of the hostile Sioux who frequented the area—to ignore this threat completely would have been extremely foolish. Yet it had not deterred either explorer from traveling through the well-known Sioux territory between Pembina and Turtle Mountain. Transportation by Red River cart, as their Métis guides could have told them, would have been difficult through some of the south country but, with a few exceptions, possible. Neither could they have seen the lack of firewood, of which the Métis would also have been aware, as a deterrent, for the explorers knew full well the utility of buffalo chips. In short, southwestern Saskatchewan posed few hazards that differed from those the explorers would have encountered elsewhere on their journeys across the West.

Their outright refusal to investigate the southwest probably lies in what their Métis guides told them about its lack of water and grass cover. Both 1857 and 1858 were very dry years. The little grass left by the buffalo had been cropped to the ground by a scourge of grasshoppers. Neither expedition's horses would have survived long without grass. Even in the best of years, most of the available surface water was so alkaline it was hardly fit to drink. The impracticality of the traverse, with the presumed uselessness of the country for agricultural purposes, probably explains why neither Palliser nor Dawson and Hind undertook a more southerly excursion. Because of this, southwestern Saskatchewan remained a land unknown to non-natives despite the scientific attention lavished on the North-West between 1857 and 1860.

Economy, Ecology, and Culture

The robe and bone trades inexorably drew the Native Peoples of the plains into a broader economic orbit than the one that had attracted and held their woodland and parkland counterparts for two centuries. This was, first, the orbit of Europe, where the great trading companies ultimately sold their furs and, second, the orbit of the eastern metropolises of the United States and Canada that bought up the robes, hides, and bones of the buffalo during the latter part of the nineteenth century. Imperialism, even in the most apolitical sense of the term, was the root of the matter. Whoever controlled the plains economy indirectly controlled the plains environment and culture as well.

The Native Peoples and the Métis, attracted by the immediate gains of the trade, were in the vanguard of the assault on the very resources that gave their cultures meaning. In turning their profound knowledge of the regional ecosystem to monetary advantage, they quickly depleted the natural resources of the plains to satisfy a far-off, metropolitan-based demand that they scarcely understood. This, not the land sales fever of the succeeding railway era, represents the first economic boom-and-bust of the northern plains region and shows clearly the basic connection between perception of a resource and the nature of its exploitation. And, as in every boom, the economic shift produced a few winners and many losers. Here it was the Native Peoples and the Métis who became marginal people in the very land they had so recently dominated.

THE RANGE

THREE
At Home on the Range

Elimination of the buffalo hastened development of the northern Great Plains as rangeland. The rotational grazing of domesticated animals has been a part of human history for at least ten thousand years. Traditionally, those who follow this way of life have little scientific knowledge of the land they inhabit, yet they manage its resources on a sustained basis, never stretching the grazing capacity of the land beyond its ability to recover. As practiced on the northern Great Plains, however, the grazing of cattle was more concerned with short-term profits than with sustained land use. To the ranchers, the open grasslands that stretched to every horizon in southwestern Saskatchewan were an investment frontier possessing an abundant, renewable resource in nutritious, sun-cured grass. When they surveyed their imported herds of cattle and horses, they saw them primarily as an efficient means of converting that rich grass to negotiable cash.

The ranching industry that developed in southwestern Saskatchewan after 1880 was part of a much broader pattern of economic investment on the northern Great Plains. That investment, in turn, was linked to the construction of railways that transported cattle and beef to market. The Canadian Pacific Railway provided an outlet for eastern manufactured goods while hauling unprocessed natural resources in the opposite direction. Cattle were the most important early commodity shipped out of the plains, for the growing urban centers of North America and Europe had a voracious appetite for beef. Western ranching could not have succeeded as a commercial enterprise without the demand of those distant markets and the technology to reach them. Indeed, it is fair to say that the marketplace and the newly arrived railway had more to do with the transformation of the plains than the ranchers themselves; they were merely the agents of a new economic regime.

Long dismissed as the northern extension of the Great American Desert, the country west of Wood Mountain underwent an economic reappraisal in 1880 that did much to reshape public opinion. The botanist John Macoun, who had been out West several times during the 1870s, skirted this land when he studied the Assiniboine and Qu'Appelle valleys in the summer of 1879. The following year, he returned at the request of the government to conduct a detailed examination of the country south and west of the Missouri Coteau. His investigation took him to Fort Ellice, across the Souris River plains, along the Coteau itself, through the badlands west of Moose Mountain, and up the south branch of the Saskatchewan River, with an excursion to the Cypress Hills and nearby Fort Walsh. A thriving farmstead some thirty miles (50 km) northwest of the Cypress Hills on a branch of Maple Creek particularly impressed him. While his endorsement of the core of Palliser's triangle as an agricultural paradise was less enthusiastic than his opinion of the verdant Assiniboine and Qu'Appelle valleys, Macoun nonetheless concluded that most, if not all, of this dry land was suitable for farming.

Macoun reached this astonishing conclusion by denying that semi-aridity alone was of much consequence in determining farming potential. Of greater relevance, in his view, was the volume of precipitation received during the growing season. If sufficient rain fell in those months, conditions during the balance of the year mattered little to the success of agriculture. The Dominion government, eager to entice investors into building a transcontinental railway, wholeheartedly embraced Macoun's views, saying officially that the "so-called American Desert which extends northerly into Canadian territory, is proved to have no existence at all."[1]

While the kernel of truth in Macoun's reinterpretation of the south country could do nothing to alter its fundamental unsuitability for cereal agriculture, official broadcast of such information would have a significant long-term impact on public perceptions of the region. Meanwhile, it would be part of the ranchers' frontier.

The Nascent Ranching Industry

Without the buffalo, its only significant trade commodity in the presettlement era, southwestern Saskatchewan regressed to the status of an economic backwater between 1874 and 1884. Cattle ranching emerged slowly as the only new economic activity of significance.

The first, and for several years the only, people to act upon the local potential for raising cattle were Métis and French-Canadians whose ability to earn a livelihood from freighting, provisioning, or trading had eroded decisively since the mid-1870s. But those who adopted cattle ranching as one means of earning their livelihood found it difficult to profit much from their new enterprise. Despite the growing demand for beef on the plains, southwestern Saskatchewan itself offered few significant markets for cattle.

To the west were the Cypress Hills, part of the economic hinterland of Fort Benton, Montana. The major settlement, Fort Walsh, which had been established in 1875 by the North-West Mounted Police, was by 1880 a settlement of 150 Mounted Police, 40 non-native settlers, and 20 Métis. The population of local Native Peoples fluctuated; it is clear their presence at certain times of the year was significant. In 1882, for example, the Mounted Police distributed a total of $31,000 in treaty funds at Fort Walsh. At $5 per head, the payment represented a peak Native population of more than 6000 people. This number would not have included any remaining Sioux, who received no annuities from the Canadian government.

The American firm of T. C. Power and Company operated a trading post at Fort Walsh for eight years (1875–83) and did a lucrative business with the local people. In the 1890s, however, the Department of Indian Affairs had sufficient support in the field to confine the Native Peoples to their reserves, which were located to the north of the main line of the Canadian Pacific Railway. While the Department remained a major customer for beef elsewhere on the plains, the lack of Indian reserves in the south limited local opportunities and trade at Fort Walsh declined.

To the south and east, the Métis at Wood Mountain were the focus of economic activity. In 1880, 42 Métis families, representing more than 300 people, resided within about a forty-mile (65-km) radius. Most of the 2900 American Sioux who came to the area in 1877 had since returned to the United States, but about 100 lodges (perhaps as many as 800 people) remained at Wood Mountain under the leadership of Sitting Bull during the winter months. In the summer the Sioux were itinerant, camping along the Frenchman River and hunting south of the international boundary.

Wood Mountain was also the site of a post the North-West Mounted Police had opened in 1877 to deal with the Sioux crisis and other border issues. In addition, the Mounted Police set up three minor outposts between Fort Walsh and Wood Mountain. By November of 1877, the Wood Mountain post consisted of sixteen men, with six more at the Pinto Horse Butte outpost. Together they had twenty-eight horses. In 1878 the Wood Mountain complement rose to twenty-two and then, one year later, to twenty-seven men. For a brief period, their needs, with those of the Native Peoples and Métis, commanded the attention of no fewer than six trading concerns, including that of Jean-Louis Légaré, an enterprising French-Canadian who had worked previously on the plains with independent traders George Fisher and Antoine Ouellette. In 1880, following a devastating prairie fire that destroyed all the grass and timber on Wood Mountain, most Native Peoples and Métis moved to the Frenchman River or the Milk River south of the 49th parallel.

After the fire, other residents of Wood Mountain relocated to a small Métis community called Willow Bunch, which had been established in 1870 following an earlier serious fire at Wood Mountain. Légaré soon became a leading merchant and community leader. In addition to providing work for many local hands in his own trading establishment, he convinced Lieutenant-Governor Edgar Dewdney to hire Métis scouts to patrol the 49th parallel, took a leading role in convincing Sitting Bull and his followers to return to the United States in 1881 and, four years later, organized a contingent of loyal Métis to assist government troops in the fight against Louis Riel in the North Saskatchewan country. Through the efforts of merchants such as Légaré, Willow Bunch quickly assumed the mantle of metropolis from Wood Mountain.

Willow Bunch, with its thirty families of Métis, emerged as the hub of the first tentative ranching operations in southwestern Saskatchewan. Légaré took a leading role in this development. In 1884, he trailed in forty-five head of cattle from Manitoba and pastured them at Willow Bunch. Two years later, a French-Canadian named Pascal Bonneau started a small ranch in the area with the help of his three sons: Trefflé, Joseph, and Pascal. Bonneau's original herd comprised four horses and four cattle. With capital investments in stock came a new attitude toward property, and in the spring of 1886 Légaré orchestrated a local petition to the Dominion government for a land survey, which was carried out on a limited basis in both the Wood Mountain and Willow Bunch districts later that year.

Although little is known about the size of the markets served by the early ranchers, logic suggests that the Mounted Police and the Department of Indian Affairs, mainly through their representatives at Fort Walsh and Wood Mountain, were the principal buyers of beef. The ranchers also dealt in hay. In 1888, for example, three individuals in Wood Mountain sold seventy-five tons (68 tonnes) of hay to the Wood Mountain detachment of the Mounted Police. The sale of oats for horse feed may also have been important, although no direct evidence of such transactions seems to exist. In addition, some ranchers derived supplementary income from cutting and hauling fence rails for the Mounted Police. They also contracted out their services as freighters, guides, translators, and patrolmen.

Limited local markets and the absence of a significant transportation infrastructure in southwestern Saskatchewan obliged these first ranchers to operate on a small scale. The growth of the ranching industry was slow, for a time the local population actually declined, and the impact of the new economic regime on the environment remained negligible for about a decade. Nonetheless, these early Métis ranchers were harbingers of a fundamentally different economic order in the south country.

Growing Markets

Southwestern Saskatchewan did not remain on the periphery of the investment frontier for long. Industrializing Europe could not produce enough meat to feed its rapidly growing urban population. As a result, the vast, sparsely populated grasslands of the world were quickly conscripted into livestock production. During the 1860s live cattle (and sheep) were shipped from Argentina, Australia, and the United States to Europe to meet the demand, and after 1879 refrigerated ships provided a new and cheaper means of transporting meat to market. Railways linked the distant inland ranching country of North America with the ocean freighters that now routinely carried cattle overseas. Southwestern Saskatchewan was drawn into this vast outside market after 1883 when the Canadian Pacific Railway crossed the prairies just to the north.

Britain was the most important market to stock-raisers in North America, and the pattern of exports was the same for all producers on the continent: exports rose spectacularly after 1880 and continued to rise for the next two decades before falling prior to the start of the Great War. During the 1890s, as ranching found its legs in southwestern Saskatchewan, Canadian cattle exports to Great Britain hovered around one-quarter of all British beef imports.

The reason for this demand was an outbreak of anthrax in Britain in the 1860s that substantially reduced British herds after 1869. European countries could not fill the demand, and the British favored North American livestock because they believed that they were less likely to carry disease. This attitude changed somewhat in 1878, when the discovery of pleuro-pneumonia in an American shipment caused the British to insist that all American cattle be slaughtered at their port of entry within ten days of arrival. This meant that American shippers incurred additional holding and slaughtering costs once their cattle reached Great Britain. For a time, this bestowed preferential treatment upon Canadian cattle, which continued to be permitted to enter the country as live stock. Their competitive price advantage, and a British preference for fresh beef, drove up demand for Canadian cattle until pleuro-pneumonia was found in a herd arriving from Montreal in 1892. Despite the new need to slaughter Canadian cattle on arrival, British demand for Canadian beef remained high.

Before 1882, there were effectively no federal regulations governing stock-raising in the North-West. It mattered little, for so few settlers had taken up land that security of tenure, let alone crowding of the range, was not an issue. The situation changed rapidly after construction of the Canadian Pacific Railway. Astute eastern Canadian stockmen, such as Senator Matthew Cochrane of Quebec, saw the potential for large-scale ranching in the unsettled West and petitioned Prime Minister John A. Macdonald for appropriate legislation. Together, Cochrane, Macdonald, and the minister of agriculture, John Pope, worked out amendments to the Dominion Lands Act that gave prospective ranchers the catalyst they needed to launch a successful livestock industry in western Canada.

The terms of the leasehold legislation of December 1881 were generous. They provided for leases of up to 100,000 acres (40,500 ha) for a term of twenty-one years. Rent was to be assessed at a rate of one cent per acre per year (2.5 cents/ha/year). In return, the lessee was obligated to graze one head of cattle for every ten acres (4 ha) of leased land within three years of being granted a lease. Lessees also had the option of purchasing a "home farm and corral" of unspecified size for two dollars per acre ($5/ha). They could bring cattle into the country free of duty. The government reserved only the right to cancel any lease without reason on two years' notice.

The government's liberal grazing lease policy encouraged rapid development of ranching. In 1882 alone, Ottawa received 154 applications for leases covering more than four million acres (1,620,000 ha). Most of the requests were for leaseholds in the Rocky Mountain foothills region south of Calgary. Demand continued to climb until the sobering North-West Rebellion of 1885, but when the uprising was over interest rose again. By 1887—the high point of the leasehold era—ten million acres (4,050,000 ha) were under lease. During more or less the same period, the estimated number of cattle on the Canadian range shot up from 9000 to 100,000.

Southwestern Saskatchewan was drawn gradually into this new economic regime. Once the railway arrived, it did not take long for the international firm of T. C. Power and Company to abandon its isolated Fort Walsh trading post in favor of one at the new railway siding of Maple Creek. In 1884 a telegraph line was installed between Wood Mountain and the new railway divisional point of Moose Jaw. Wood Mountain rancher William Ogle later recalled how crucial this line was to the local people in getting "important news of the world."[2] He also delighted at the ease with which liquor could be obtained via the railway. The less well-heeled were more interested in the prospects the new line presented for cattle ranching after 1883. Employment as a telegraph lineman was critical to Fred Brown's modest entry into the local ranching community. Later, Brown would also obtain the first contract for mail delivery between Moose Jaw and Wood Mountain.

Daniel Webster Marsh and his nephew Horace A. Greeley, formerly connected with the T. C. Power and Company post at Fort Walsh, obtained a leasehold of nearly nine thousand acres (3645 ha) near Maple Creek in 1886 and brought in three hundred cattle to fatten. The Power brothers themselves operated a 24,500-acre (9915-ha) ranch near the Cypress Hills. In 1886, John H. Conrad of Fort Benton stocked a 200,000-acre (81,000-ha) lease in the same area with two thousand head of cattle. The railway was critical to their success. Because there were no American lines nearby in Montana, large-scale Montana ranchers negotiated a special agreement with Canadian authorities to drive their cattle to the Maple Creek railhead between 1884 and 1886. This arrangement simplified the shipment of Montana stock to the booming Chicago market.

Nearer Wood Mountain, renewed investment in ranching began at the same time, if not on the same scale. Former North-West Mounted Policemen such as Edward "Buffalo" Allen and Fred Brown started small cattle ranches between 1886 and 1890. We do not know the size of Allen's investment, but Brown is recorded as having trailed in some 150 Montana cattle in 1890. Invariably these men took on wage employment as well, again implying that the local market for cattle throughout the 1880s was simply too small and the distance to the railway too great for them to devote themselves exclusively to stock-raising. Their failure to apply for any grazing leases may also point to their limited degree of commitment to the enterprise, although it must be said that the lack of competition for grass in southwestern Saskatchewan made leases largely unnecessary.

Border Crossings

There were always those, however, who implicitly understood the economic impact of the railway and did not hesitate to predict a ranching future for the whole south country. These were often people from outside the region. For example, in 1886 J. S. Dennis, the surveyor-general of Canada, crossed the prairies and reported enthusiastically that

> The cattle ranching industry is making wonderfully rapid strides. . . . Bands of cattle were visited at the mouth of the Red Deer River, at Medicine Hat, and at Wood Mountain, all of which were found in flourishing condition. . . .The generally accepted theory has been that the grazing area was restricted to the south-western portion of the Territories, but the present indications are that a very much larger area is well adapted for grazing. I am of the opinion that all the country in the vicinity of, and south of the Canadian Pacific Railway line to the international boundary, west of Moose Jaw, is more or less adapted for [sic] cattle ranching.[3]

Factors other than environmental reappraisals made southwestern Saskatchewan increasingly attractive as well. Grazing pressures on the American side of the line created a demand for local grass. The American experience with cattle on the northern plains had begun much earlier than Canada's. During the 1860s the hardrock mining and placer gold camps of Idaho, British Columbia, and western Montana had created such a large market for beef that the herds quickly spilled over onto the grasslands to the east, occupying a new grazing belt some two hundred miles (320 km) wide. Demand for beef was high and there were huge profits to be made by shrewd investors. Both start-up and operational costs for a ranch south of the 49th parallel were modest in relation to the climbing price of beef. Reports of 40 percent profit margins were common. Though likely inflated to entice investors, the reports nonetheless served to attract significant capital to the industry. The actual return, particularly as new investors joined the throng, was probably closer to 25 or 30 percent—still a huge gain. While American investors led this stampede to the plains, much capital also came from Great Britain, where disease during the 1860s had drastically reduced herds and increased prices. Once railways began to penetrate the West, it became possible to ship cattle to the rising cities of the east or even overseas with little difficulty. The United States government also purchased some 50,000 head each year to provide beef rations on its Indian reservations.

Unable to envision a drop in demand, and awash in investment capital, American ranchers continued to build up their herds to the point where they ruined the Montana range, and others, through overgrazing. The impact did not stop there. According to historian Rodmand Paul:

> Cattlemen were slow to acknowledge that continued exclusive reliance on the natural grasses was no longer safe, that they must provide supplementary hay and feed or risk killing their stock. Because they did not own the range, they disregarded warnings that the dry, overgrazed range was visibly deteriorating as the undernourished cattle attacked every growing thing. Noxious weeds were replacing the grasses, springs were being reduced to "filthy trampled mudholes," and as the cattle wandered farther and farther in their daily hunt for dwindling food and water, their hooves cut pathways down through the parched soil, thus starting "the thin edge of the wedge of erosion."[4]

By 1885, according to Joseph Nimmo, an American government statistician, there were 7.5 million head of cattle east of the Rockies and north of New Mexico and Texas. Some 600,000 of these were in Montana Territory. The grazing pressure of the stock was so intense that by the mid-1880s many observers perceived the Montana range as crowded beyond its capacity. Under such circumstances, Montana cattle soon found their way into Canada and onto the grasslands of the southwestern Saskatchewan.

American ranchers did not hesitate to request grazing leases from the Canadian government. By the end of 1886, they had asked for and obtained nearly one-fifth of all the leases held in western Canada. These leases extended eastward in a thin band from the foothills to the Manitoba border, and a few were located in southwestern Saskatchewan. The first American herd known to have been brought into that territory was that of the St. Louis–based Home Land and Cattle Company (the "N-N" brand). In 1886, following a summer of drought, they trailed some 6000 cattle and 250 horses into Wood Mountain and established a base camp about six miles (10 km) west of the North-West Mounted Police post. The winter of 1886–87 was extremely harsh, however, and devastated herds on both sides of the line. The "N-N" herd was no exception. By 1888 Mounted Police at Wood Mountain were reporting that "there are no cattle left in the Wood Mountain District, those of the Home Land and Cattle Company having been removed to Rock Creek, south of the boundary line."[5] Despite the brevity of this incursion, it proved the feasibility of such transborder operations and foretold the far deeper relationship that would soon develop between American cattle and Canadian grass.

Farther north, nearer the main line of the Canadian Pacific Railway, a British baronet by the name of Sir John Lister-Kaye launched an operation in 1888 that would long have consequences for the entire region. Lister-Kaye invested heavily in ten 10,000-acre (4050-ha) "ranch-farms," as he called them, extending along the main line from Rush Lake west to the foothills. Three ranch-farms were located near the new town of Swift Current: one at Rush Lake, a second at Gull Lake, and a third immediately south of Swift Current. In 1888 Lister-Kaye imported 5800 head of cattle from the Powder River Ranch Company in Wyoming—whose assets were liquidated after the severe winter of 1886–87—and many horses, sheep, and pigs from other North American sources. The Powder River cattle had been branded with the "76" brand and Lister-Kaye left them that way after the purchase. Henceforth, Lister-Kaye's operation would be known as the "76" and its cattle would repeatedly stray into grazing country flanking the Frenchman River.

A second weaker wave of interest in bringing cattle to southwestern Saskatchewan arrived around 1890. It was Canadian in origin and modest in scale. In the Wood Mountain district, several new investors brought in small herds. R. and J. B. Thompson trailed in 330 cattle from Fort Pelly in 1892 and established themselves at Elm Creek. Within the next three years, three other Canadian ranchers arrived with small herds. A former North-West Mounted Police constable, Bushby, and his partner proposed bringing cattle in from Manitoba as well. Independent trader-turned-rancher Jean-Louis Légaré maintained the largest operation in the area in the mid-

1890s. After another hard winter in 1893–94, he sold 1125 of his cattle to the Bonneau family to concentrate on horse ranching. In 1892 the commanding officer of the Wood Mountain detachment of the North-West Mounted Police said that Willow Bunch ranchers alone were raising four to five hundred horses. Moderate investors in cattle ranching, such as Marsh and Greeley, seem to have been unable to weather the hard winters. They first cut their leased holdings by nearly two-thirds and then reduced them even further. Only those with deeper pockets, such as the Power brothers and the Conrads, retained their large leases in the area.

Demand for range in southwestern Saskatchewan remained low during the last decade of the nineteenth century. Sufficient time had not yet passed to rebuild the American herds lost during the winter of 1886–87 and many ranchers continued to export cattle to pay down their debts. Nor was the quest for grass what it had been in neighboring Montana. In 1888, the United States government severely reduced the size of its Blackfeet reservation in northwestern Montana, freeing some twenty million acres (8,100,000 ha) of prime grazing land for ranchers in the bargain. Overall demand for Canadian grazing land peaked in 1887 and never again reached the same level. Despite this, American cattle continued to cross the border, much to the increasing irritation of the local North-West Mounted Police officers who patrolled the area.

A distinct disregard for Canadian law characterized American economic interest in southwestern Saskatchewan during the 1890s. Although Americans were quick to obtain leases in other parts of the Canadian range, southwestern Saskatchewan was almost all unleased land and American cattle commonly grazed across the line with little thought given to Canadian sovereignty or local concerns. The cattle ranged north from the large ranches of Montana's Valley County and made their way up the Milk and the Frenchman rivers into what remained an unsettled and largely unpatrolled country.

At first American cattle grazed in southwestern Canada with complete impunity. As late as 1892, Superintendent A. B. Perry of the North-West Mounted Police referred to the entire district west of the Missouri Coteau as an "uninhabited, almost unknown country . . . stretching away south to the Missouri River."[6] Regular patrols of the border west from Wood Mountain and east from Frenchman River began only in 1893 when the Dominion government enacted a quarantine on all American cattle entering Canada. This was in response to the pleuro-pneumonia scare and its potential effect on exports to the important British market. The Mounted Police were sorely tried in their efforts to keep a watch on the vast, unpopulated territory. It was such rough country, in fact, that few horses had the stamina needed for the long patrol.

As the years passed, the onerous quarantine patrol was to remain one of the Mounted Policemen's least popular duties. Superintendent Perry, traveling through the district in 1894 with one regular patrol, noted an American roundup of 250 cattle along the Frenchman River. He gently chided his superior that "it is interesting to note that the 'round-up' was composed of practical cowboys furnished with eight to ten horses each, and that we demand almost the same work from our inexperienced men with only a single horse."[7]

Reports of American cattle ranging as far north as Crane Lake and Old Wives Lake became common. In response, Officer Herchmer reported:

[I] engaged a line rider who will assist the police to get them [the American cattle] out of Canada. None of the American owners of cattle that infest Wood Mountain neighborhood keep a line rider, or even attempt to keep their cattle south, and I would again urge your department the desirability of notifying such owners, that they must keep their stock out of Canada, failing which they should be rounded up and a fine imposed, otherwise they will continue to keep their cattle in our territory whenever possible.[8]

If the experience of 1895–96 is considered typical of conditions at the end of the century—and Mounted Police reports suggest it can be—thousands of American cattle ranged illegally throughout the country from the border to the Canadian Pacific Railway on the north. In December of 1895, W. H. White-Fraser of the North-West Mounted Police reported three thousand cattle from the Montana-based Bloom Cattle Company near Eastend. Another one thousand head were found near Willow Bunch, much to the consternation of the elder Pascal Bonneau. Smaller herds owned by various American companies ranged through the same country all year long. To make matters worse, when the Americans did round up their herds, they frequently took only the best cattle across the line, leaving the inferior stock to fend for themselves in Canada.

The situation had not changed by 1897. In July some four thousand American cattle were rounded up by the North-West Mounted Police in the Maple Creek district and driven across the border, only to have three thousand return within two weeks. Besides consuming valuable grass and water, the inferior American bulls left behind by the American ranchers bred with Canadian cows. "The result," according to the Mounted Police, "is small calf crops, and many young heifers irretrievably injured, and if continued, stock raising in the southern country will be disastrously checked."[9] So unremitting was this American cattle "invasion" that the Mounted Police eventually suggested, more out of exasperation than common sense, that the entire 49th parallel be fenced. The frustration of the Mounted Police reflected their diminishing ability to enforce the law in such a vast unpeopled district. The Wood Mountain detachment, for example, declined from twenty-three men in 1894 to only three in 1898. Boundary patrols henceforth became more irregular and ineffectual than ever.

What the Mounted Police saw as blatant American disregard for Canadian law can better be ascribed to the pressure all ranchers, regardless of nationality, were feeling around the turn of the century. Farm settlement was rapidly overtaking the range. In Montana, well before 1900, proponents of dryland farming were pushing up against the semi-arid Benchland district north of the Musselshell River. The real farm boom would not come for another four or five years, but it was already plain that the days of the unrestricted range were fast fading. The same was true of the Canadian plains. Extension of the Calgary and Edmonton branch of the Canadian Pacific Railway south from Calgary to Fort Macleod in 1891 opened that ranching enclave to settlement. Confronted by the inevitable, some ranchers sold out, others purchased part of their leaseholds and became stockmen, and still others shifted the focus of their operations farther east into the drier country on either side of the Cypress Hills that held little attraction for farmers. One result was greater pressure on the comparatively unused rangelands of southwestern Saskatchewan.

Relocation to, or expansion into, such thinly populated areas made good business sense in the last years of the nineteenth century. Demand for North American beef remained strong and prices were accordingly high. The restriction of the range caused by the influx of farm settlers was offset to some extent by their demand for both beef and horses. Between 1896 and 1906, the number of farm settlers in Canada grew from 21,716 to 189,000. In 1913 this figure would peak at more than 400,000. In addition, prairie towns sprang up every eight to ten miles (15 km) along an increasingly dense railway network throughout the prairies. Western cities boomed as well. Strong foreign and domestic demand continued to make ranching a shrewd investment.

Whereas the grass of southwestern Saskatchewan had been used almost incidentally before 1900, after the turn of the century it became a commodity much sought after, especially by the Americans. Some local ranchers, such as the Bonneaus, significantly increased their herds during this period. In 1900, the elder Pascal Bonneau had four hundred cattle and four hundred horses on his ranch, and his son Pascal ran a herd of five to six thousand head. Their investments were dwarfed, however, by the capital available to and wielded by Montana ranchers. In 1900, The Cresswell Cattle Company brought thirty thousand cattle up from Oklahoma and distributed them from its headquarters near Medicine Hat. After 1902, the

"Turkey Track," as this firm was known from the peculiar look of its brand, operated a ranch near Vanguard on Notukeu Creek and had line camps at Seventy Mile Crossing (Val Marie) and near the point where the French-man River crossed the border into the United States. In the same year the Bloom Land and Cattle Company (better known as the "T-Bar Down" ranch) came to southwestern Saskatchewan and established a line camp at Fifty Mile Crossing (Eastend) that oversaw the grazing of ten thousand cattle during the summer season. Significantly, owner Frank Bloom in-structed his scouts on the range to look for two townships of land with no settlers on it. A smaller American outfit, the "Z-X" ranch, owned by the Enright brothers and J. C. Strong of Montana, trailed in fifteen hundred cattle to the Frenchman River valley in 1906. The three outfits operated more or less from the border north to the "76" range on Swift Current Creek, and from Wood Mountain on the east to Eastend on the west. Effec-tively, these American ranchers controlled all the grazing land in south-western Saskatchewan after 1902.

American ranchers saw southwestern Saskatchewan as a land of free grass similar to the one they had enjoyed for many years south of the line. Some took out leases that covered small parts of their operations, but for the most part these ranchers remained unbound by the leasehold regula-tions of the Dominion Lands Act. No one seems to have given this ar-rangement a second thought for southwestern Saskatchewan continued to be perceived by most as a wasteland as far as cereal agriculture was con-cerned. Pascal Bonneau's daughter Marie remembers that its reputation was so poor that the Canadian Pacific Railway scheduled its trains to cross the country between Regina and the Alberta border at night, lest prospec-tive settlers glimpse its dismal character. As long as better arable land was available elsewhere on the prairies, few farmers seriously entertained the idea of settling in the south country.

The land remained almost totally unfenced, enabling local ranchers to operate their spreads according to the American tradition of the free range. This saw cattle thrown out onto the range in spring to graze unmolested until the fall roundup. Much of the time the ranchers rarely knew where most of their cattle were. As the cattle were free to follow the best grazing, ranchers gave little thought to putting up hay to see their herds through a hard winter. The dangers in this approach became apparent to the Ameri-can newcomers in 1903–04 when severe winter weather followed serious fall prairie fires and a hard early frost, leaving the cattle with nothing to eat. The effect was devastating. Around Willow Bunch, the Métis lost all of their cattle. Three years later, in 1906–07, even worse winter conditions caused the loss of an estimated 60 to 70 percent of all cattle in southwest-ern Saskatchewan. H. S. Jones, who crossed the range from Stone Pile to the "T-Bar Down" ranch in the early summer of 1907 and encountered nothing but bovine carcasses, said it looked "like a big battlefield."[10] Ranchers put the remaining stock, which were of poor quality, on the market to recover some of their losses but a worldwide recession had already driven down prices and this new flood of cattle produced another sharp, if temporary, decline in prices. This setback marked the end of ranching's absolute dominance of the area's economy.

The Impending Threat

The hard winter of 1906–07 was the symbolic end of ranching's first phase in southwestern Saskatchewan and indeed on the Great Plains as a whole. Yet in Canada, it was the Dominion Lands Act of 1908 that effectively ended the era of free range and, with it, the *laissez-faire* attitude that had prevailed among ranchers toward the grassland environment.

In 1904 Canadians reelected the Liberal administration of Sir Wilfrid Laurier to a second term in office. The years since 1896 had been excellent for the country as a whole. Western Canada, in particular, was booming due to Laurier's strong support for agricultural immigration and settlement as a means of solidifying transcontinental unity through closer economic integration. Prices for farm commodities were high, unemployment low, and optimism universal. Seldom had any Dominion government enjoyed such national support. It came as no surprise that Laurier's new administration saw the completion of western farm settlement as its central policy. The Liberal Party, unlike the Conservative administration that had established the original leasehold regulations in December of 1881, was the farmers' party.

Amendments to the Dominion Lands Act in 1908 legitimized the drive for dense farm settlement across the entire prairie West. Homesteaders had already taken up much of the land available north of the Canadian Pacific main line. The prospect of two more transcontinental railways through that region, with the many feeder lines each planned, promised to complete settlement of the northern Great Plains quickly and on the compact pattern anticipated by Ottawa. It was south of the main line, where the semi-arid character of the land worked against dense settlement, that the Dominion government took special measures to encourage farming in order to complete settlement of the West. The 1908 amendments made it possible for settlers to homestead not 160 acres (65 ha), as happened elsewhere, but 320 (130 ha) by virtue of preemption of an adjoining quarter. Dominion officials felt that only larger farms, operated according to the proven principles of dryland agriculture, could succeed in the south country of Saskatchewan and Alberta.

Sectional land surveys were the key to making homesteads available to incoming settlers, yet when the 1908 amendments passed much of southwestern Saskatchewan had only been surveyed down to the township level. The demand for land south of the line was so great, however, that this failed to discourage farm settlement in any but the driest parts of the interior where many of the largest ranches were located. By 1913 farms hemmed in most ranches. New towns such as Gergovia, Reliance, Coriander, and Hillandale sprang up to serve the farmers' needs and a pattern of roads aligned to the sectional grid began to connect the new urban communities.

Ranchers who did not to wish to liquidate their outfits could respond to such settlement pressure in only two ways, neither of which pleased them. They could purchase land outright, but even those few with sufficient means to do this were restricted to a maximum of 320 acres (130 ha). Alternatively, they could lease land from the Dominion government, but this still involved some cost and offered no long-term security of tenure. Importantly, leased land had to be classified by the government as unfit for cereal agriculture. The pressure of farm settlement being what it was, the government classified less and less land as such. No rancher could be certain that his range would not be reclassified when his current lease expired.

The devastating winter of 1906–07, taken together with this new insecurity of tenure, encouraged the large American outfits to sell out. By 1910 the "Turkey Track," the "T-Bar Down," and the "76" were all in the hands of Winnipeg-based Gordon, Ironsides and Fares, a large meatpacking concern. This move resembled the consolidation of ranches undertaken by their main competitor, Patrick Burns, in Alberta just a few years before. Little is known about the operations of Gordon, Ironsides and Fares, but it is believed that even as late as 1912 the company had not obtained leases on any of the land it grazed. Consolidation of the three largest ranches in the area freed a considerable amount of range that was quickly occupied by many smaller ranch operators.

In 1912 there were nearly six hundred ranch leaseholds in Saskatchewan, situated mainly between Saskatchewan Landing and the 49th parallel, west and south of Moose Jaw. The scale of the typical operation stands in marked contrast to the Gordon, Ironsides and Fares outfit. The average number of livestock on the 381 ranches that filed returns in 1912 was about 90 horses, 150 cattle, and nearly 200 sheep. While horses and cattle were fairly evenly distributed throughout the southwest, sheep were confined to the Crane Lake, Carmichael, Forres, Kincorth, Tompkins, and Seward districts close to the railway line. It was rare to find them in any numbers on ranches farther south. If we can judge from the names of the lessees, corporate ranches were the exception; individuals or brothers owned most outfits. After the "die-out" winter of 1906–07, then, ranching in the southwest returned to its origins as a small-scale enterprise.[11]

The market for livestock remained quite buoyant until about 1920. Between 1907 and 1913, there was a particularly strong demand for draft horses as incoming farmers broke the prairie. R. D. Symons of the "76" observed that a shift into horse production began following the winter of 1906–07, which horses survived much better than cattle, and was then further stimulated by farm settlement. The growth of prairie cities, with a general decline in the number of cattle after the winter of 1906–07, ensured that the market for livestock remained generally good. When the United States lifted its tariff on foreign commercial cattle in 1913, Canadian ranchers also had access to a new and potentially large market via the stockyards of Chicago and St. Paul. In short, ranchers had many sound reasons to remain in business despite setbacks caused by the hard winter of 1906–07.

An Industry Under Siege

In 1909 the provincial Department of Agriculture circulated a questionnaire that captured the prevailing sentiment of beleaguered livestock breeders, ranchers, and buyers:

> The ranchers complained bitterly of the encroachments of the homesteaders, the resulting introduction of herd law, and the curtailment of range and water privileges. Many of them assert that a well-established and long-tried industry is being destroyed for the sale of a precarious one—as they consider farming in the semi-arid south-western portion of the province to be. They appear to consider their industry doomed, and statistics justify their contention.[12]

A Mounted Police report observed in 1912 that "ranching in this part of the province will soon be a thing of the past."[13] However real the threat, ranchers responded moderately by focusing on changes to existing stock-raising practices and on the application of political pressure.

The physical constriction of the range mattered little to the remaining ranchers in the southwest for the smaller herd size after 1907 meant that pasture requirements were low and it had become increasingly common for ranchers to stack wild hay from sloughs to see their cattle through the winter. One 1907 report noted that a serious prairie fire had destroyed many haystacks along the Frenchman River. Three years later, land surveyor C. F. Miles commented favorably on the haystacks of settlers south of Willow Bunch.

Nonetheless, there were those who continued to reject the need for hay. Jean-Louis Légaré was among them. In his reply to a 1909 government questionnaire, Légaré proudly pointed out he had not fed hay to his cattle during either of the last two winters. As time went on, however, attitudes such as Légaré's became a minority view in the southwest. Haying became so common, in fact, that the newly appointed Livestock Commission began recording the size of the hay crop for the province as a whole and the average yield and price per ton by crop district. On the "Z-X" ranch on the lower Frenchman River, irrigation of hay meadows and tame hay crops began as early as 1907. By the start of the Great War, Frank Cross, who ranched on the north branch of the river, had become something of a local exemplar for his dedicated cultivation of tame hay crops such as timothy, brome grass, and Red Top. Not surprisingly, outside such oases, the yield of both wild and tame hay in the dry southwestern part of Saskatchewan was usually among the lowest in the province, with prices correspondingly above the provincial average.

Local ranchers began to take winter feeding seriously during the war years at least partly because livestock prices had never been so high. There was also a sharp rise in demand for horses, although as the demand was largely military it lasted only as long as the conflict itself. Similarly, cattle prices were closely tied to wartime demand. In 1914 the average Winnipeg price for a good quality butcher steer, weighing between one thousand and twelve hundred pounds (455–545 kg), was $7.20 per hundredweight ($7.08/50 kg). By the conclusion of the war in 1918, the price had risen a miraculous 161 percent to $11.60 per hundredweight ($11.42/50 kg).

Troublesome and costly as resolution of the feed problem was, it paled in comparison to the perceived inequity of the herd law that obliged ranchers to fence their holdings. On the surface, the issue was simple: should fencing be the responsibility of the rancher, whose stock devoured grass and grain with equal relish, or of the incoming farmer, who put temptation in the way of every horse and bovine with his annual spring seeding? Representation by population being what it is, Saskatchewan's herd law favored the farmer and became another argument for the winter feeding of stock. The matter of indiscriminate breeding complicated matters further, particularly once purebred livestock became more common. A related pound law, which had been in place since 1905, permitted the impoundment and sale of stock that strayed, causing further discontent. Some ranchers called it nothing less than legalized theft.

The conflict was not easily resolved. The provincial government's original position was that each municipality was best able to decide whether to impose a herd law and at what times of the year. As farmers quickly outnumbered ranchers in most areas of the province, the threat to the established ranching community was considerable. Yet few local authorities seemed prepared to use their power in this regard. In any event, the southwest was largely unorganized territory. The lack of a consistent policy almost ensured continuing controversy.

Finally, in 1914, the provincial Department of Agriculture appointed a three-man commission to investigate the herd law. Following hearings at Eastend, Maple Creek, Ponteix, Assiniboia, Gravelbourg, Wood Mountain, Limerick, Vanguard, Shaunavon, and Willow Bunch, during which 271 witnesses were examined, the commissioners recommended that the existing herd law be retained. Their position reflected the increasingly conventional wisdom that, in the words of one farmer, admitted "no reason why a man who proposed to go into the Ranching business should not fence against [the wanderings of] his own stock."[14]

At the same time, however, the commissioners were adamant that the law be applied more consistently. They cited cases where a single municipality provided "for herding during the summer months in one township, herding throughout the year in another, and free range throughout the year in a third."[15] This was more than any rancher, however well meaning, could accept. Nonetheless, the cost and labor of fencing the range now rested squarely with the ranching community.

Issues such as these induced the ranchers to organize for their own economic protection. In 1912 several men from southwestern Saskatchewan, including Trefflé Bonneau and William Ogle of Wood Mountain, and John D. Simpson of the "Turkey Track," joined with several ranchers from the Moose Jaw district to discuss the formation of a stockgrowers' protective association. Ironically taking comfort from the gains won recently by the Grain Growers' Association, the new group adopted the name Saskatchewan Stock Growers' Association. It dedicated itself to lobbying for what it saw as more equitable legislation and achieved some gains quickly. The Dominion government appointed a Ranching and Grazing Investigation Commission to make recommendations about new leasehold provisions. Two provincial investigations into the herd and pound laws followed. While these commissions often favored the ranching community of the southwest, there was nothing they could do to affect the weather or to stabilize the recurrent convulsions of the marketplace or to arrest the tide of farm settlement.

"The cattle industry in Saskatchewan during 1917," wrote the provincial livestock commissioner, "seems to have made greater advancement than in any former year."[16] Prices had remained high because of the war, with both foreign and local demand still strong. The only sour note was that unusually dry conditions prevailed at midsummer, threatening the maturing grain and feed crops. The rains returned that year, however, and oats yielded a respectable twenty-two bushels to the acre (54 bushels/ha).

In 1918 residents of the southwest were not so fortunate. The drought came and stayed, and the yield of oats plummeted to nine bushels per acre (22 bushels/ha). As supplies dwindled, the Dominion Live Stock Branch arranged for both hay and straw to be hauled in to the stricken south country for the winter months. Nineteen-nineteen was worse, with yields hovering around just six bushels to the acre (15 bushels/ha) and extremely short hay crops. Ranchers had no choice but to liquidate their herds. The Dominion government assisted the ranchers by arranging for cattle buyers to purchase directly from the ranchers and by encouraging the railways to continue the lower rates of stock shipments that they had introduced in 1918. The exodus of horses from the southwest was unprecedented, while shipments of cattle were higher in volume than at any time other than after the winter of 1906–07.

Farm settlers, desperate for land and convinced by ill-considered government rhetoric that cereal crops could succeed where the natural grass had failed, filled the vacuum resulting from the rapid decline in grazing. Between 1921 and 1931, the amount of improved acreage in southern rural municipalities and local improvement districts increased by an average of 41 percent. In all three local improvement districts, which took in most of the remaining ranch leases, the amount of improved acreage at least doubled.

Nineteen-twenty, the third year of the drought, coincided with the peak of beef prices. The decline that followed came as a surprise to many. Most European breeding herds had been slaughtered during the war and ranchers believed this would cause an even stronger demand for imported cattle and beef. But few had stopped to consider that the shattered economies of war-torn Europe would not have any credit with which to purchase additional livestock. As European demand slackened, as the long-standing British pleuro-pneumonia embargo continued, and as a new American tariff was imposed, prices dropped steadily before hitting bottom at $5.27 per hundredweight ($5.80/50 kg) in 1924. This was the lowest price for beef since the disastrous winter of 1906–07. With ocean freight rates high, there was little profit in shipping to the once-buoyant British market. To make matters even worse, a "meat war" erupted in Great Britain because of beef dumping by South African exporters. Shipping statistics tell the story. Canadian cattle exports to Great Britain moved down from 110,868 head in 1925 to only 8263 in 1927. As if Canadian stock-raisers did not have enough to concern them, it was widely reported that the public consumption of beef was declining steadily as well.

Throughout this period of disruption, the "76" remained the only ranch of any size in southwestern Saskatchewan. In 1917 Gordon, Ironsides and

Fares had taken out a ten-year lease of 12,000 acres (4856 ha) near Sand Lake, some of the least desirable farmland in the area. By 1923, under the management of veteran rancher T. B. Long, this range was stocked with eight hundred cattle and three thousand horses. As an isolated and fairly self-contained parcel of land, the Sand Lake lease seemed as inviolate a ranch as any in southwestern Saskatchewan.

Construction of a branch of the Canadian Pacific Railway to the new town of Val Marie (the former Seventy Mile Crossing) in 1924 shattered this illusion. It was clear immediately that the land would be opened to homesteading at the expiration of the lease in 1927. Philip Long explained the determined force that his father was up against:

> Nothing could stop those hardy pioneer farmers. Even before the CPR built the line through Shaunavon there were farmers to the south who had to haul their grain to the main line at Gull Lake. This made a haul of eighty or ninety miles [130–140 km] for some, yet they seemed to make it. The hauling was all done with horses and many of them would be on the trail a week or ten days with one load. Now that the branch line was in they still had a forty or fifty mile haul [65–80 km], but this did not seem bad at all to them. Every year saw many homesteaders, settling their roots in the rich dry-land soil. Roads through the leases were becoming deeply cut by the wheels of the heavy loaded farmer's wagons as they hauled their grain to the railroad.[17]

In the spring of 1926, when T. B. Long received notice from the Dominion government that it would not renew the "76" lease, he closed a deal on a new ranch in Montana. The ranch's 77,000 acres (31,161 ha) were immediately thrown open to homesteaders, who stood and even slept in line at the Val Marie land office overnight rather than lose their chance to file on the land. Long's son, Philip, who had grown up on the ranch, looked at the snaking line in amazement and wondered "how many of them would be disappointed and watch their dreams dry up and blow away across the rolling prairie."[18]

FOUR
From Freedom to Fences

By 1880, the Métis wintering camps and the large Native encampments were gone from the grasslands of southwestern Saskatchewan, the former rendered obsolete by elimination of the buffalo, the latter by the system of reserves. In their stead were isolated ranches that made even less visual impression on the landscape. The ranchers chose sites for their headquarters much as the Native Peoples and the Métis had selected their campsites: with respect for the prevailing winds and proximity to water. Thus hidden from view, and sheltering few inhabitants, the ranches did nothing to alleviate the deep sense of emptiness that had fallen upon the southwest. If anything, they reinforced its openness, its lonely grandeur.

Without question, southwestern Saskatchewan had become a vacant land. Under the Dominion census of 1891, much of southwestern Saskatchewan was encompassed by the Swift Current Sub-District, comprising 15,904 square miles (4,200,000 ha). Only 320 people lived in that entire tract. The population density was about one person per fifty square miles (1 person/ 12,950 ha).[1] There were not even many surveyors' stakes to hint at the new Euro-Canadian interest in the land. Until 1908, much of this newly empty land was surveyed only down to the township level, with each township comprising thirty-six sections of land, or thirty-six square miles (9325 ha).

Outward signs of their new economic regime may have been scarce, but ranchers introduced an entirely new vocabulary that redefined the land according to their own cultural requirements. In their lexicon, "bottoms" were broad valleys through which a stream flowed, "coulees" described small, V-shaped valleys that saw water only during spring runoff, small valleys without water were called "draws," and "gulches" contained dry stream beds. They knew the flats above the valley as "benches." Betraying their American origins, they reserved the word "butte" for the isolated, towering, steep-sided elevations that served as landmarks throughout the south country. Even the rivers were renamed. Most noticeably, the "White Mud" (*La Terre Blanche* to the Métis) gave way to the Frenchman, but the influence of the rancher was also evident in names such as "Hay Meadow

Creek." And the undulating grasslands that stretched away to the horizon in every direction simply became the "range." This was how one "placed" oneself in the landscape before the great homesteader rush of 1908.

Trails connected the features of this sparsely settled landscape. In contrast to the sectional roads of the farming period, trails followed the natural contours of the land. For the most part, these were likely ancient thoroughfares: a comparison of trails on nineteenth- and early twentieth-century maps shows little difference between the two. As one might expect, trails connected various points by the shortest practicable means. Unlike the farmers who succeeded them, the ranchers were unhindered by a sectional grid system that often promoted conformity over common sense.

To the unknowing, the landscape of southwestern Saskatchewan appeared seamless during the ranching era. At one level, this was true. There were no roadways and few if any lengthy fences marking the land. Nevertheless, in the minds of the cattlemen, the range was clearly demarcated, not as precise zones, but into what we might call "spheres of influence." Harry Otterson has described this division of the range as a gentleman's agreement:

> The line between the Turkey-Track and the T-Down was the Fifty Mile Crossing on the Whitemud, then north-west across the present town of Instow to the Swift Current [Creek] at the mouth of Rock Creek; then the South Fork of Swift Current Creek marked the line between the "76" and the Cypress Hills ranchers and the T-Down around Eastend, and then south from Eastend to the Montana line. The west line [was] between the T-Down and the upriver ranches known as the Whitemud Pool, east between the Turkey-Track and the T-Down south of Fifty-Mile. The dividing [line] was on the divide where Orkney now stands.[2]

Without fences, an imagined division of the range was the only sensible way of adapting to the tendency of the herds to drift with the weather, the quality of the grass, and the availability of water. This perspective on the land implied a view based less on leasehold law than on the functional needs of each ranch.

In its natural luxuriance and awe-inspiring openness, it was a land that seemed to invite comment about its grazing potential. Indeed, as early as 1880 some praised southwestern Saskatchewan's stock-raising qualities above those of all other available ranges. Superintendent James Walsh of the North-West Mounted Police was one of its champions. As he explained it:

> Wood Mountain is a stock-raising as well as an agricultural district . . . horses and cattle and sheep can run the hills during the winter months without any danger of perishing by storm, by cold or by want of grass.

Highly prized as Bow River District may be as a stock-raising country, and although it may have an advantage over Wood Mountain by possessing a more extended range and having a somewhat shorter winter, yet in all other respects it cannot excel Wood Mountain. The grass of Wood Mountain is as good, if not superior, to that of Bow River, and Wood Mountain has the great advantage over Bow River by being some 400 miles [645 km] nearer the eastern markets. No part of Montana—and Montana is quoted highly as a stock-raising country—can produce a more nutritious grass, and hills and valleys more abundantly supplied, than Wood Mountain. Both valley and bench land can be cultivated.[3]

His views were reinforced strongly by those of Montana ranchers when they first came into the area from the overgrazed lands south of the border. T. B. Long, who first rode into the Cypress Hills area from Montana in 1904, was one among many who recalled that "several years growth of grass rippled in the wind, knee deep to a horse as far as the eye could see."[4] Unscientific though such observations were, they nonetheless represent shrewd, practical appraisals of southwestern Saskatchewan from the perspective of those whose livelihood depended on their intuitive grasp of range quality.

Today, the land required to graze cattle is customarily expressed as the number of acres needed to support one head of cattle for one year. The minimum number of acres that can support one head for one year without undue damage to plant cover, water supply, or soil quality is known as the theoretical carrying capacity of the land. Naturally, the carrying capacity of land varies with regional environmental conditions. Southwestern Saskatchewan is drier than most of the surrounding country and therefore able to support fewer head per acre. Because the appropriate local ratio of cattle to grass is comparatively high, the potential for environmental damage based on overstocking is also high.

Ranchers typically measure their success in terms of stock turnover and therefore want their cattle to attain mature weight as quickly as possible. When prices are high, ranchers need graze fewer animals to earn the same income, making it easier to keep the cattle-land ratio at an appropriate level. At a time of low prices, however, they may withhold their cattle from market until prices again move up, thus threatening to exceed the land's carrying capacity. If prices remain low, overstocking may damage the land. This is particularly troublesome in times of drought, which greatly reduces the ability of grass to recover from overgrazing. As captives of a global price system, ranchers tend to manage their herds with short-term profits in mind. The degree to which they observe the carrying capacity of their land, rather than the dictates of the marketplace, is critical to the survival of the grassland environment over the long term.

It is difficult to determine whether the number of cattle in southwestern Saskatchewan ever approached the land's theoretical carrying capacity before homesteaders fenced it. To do so, we would need to know several things for which no reliable data exist. First, we must know the number of head grazed per acre. While the original Dominion leasehold regulations stipulated a minimum ratio of one head per ten acres (4 ha), which was changed in 1888 to one head per twenty acres (8 ha), cattle obviously wandered at will. Second, we would need to know the turnover rate for cattle and, again, there is no information. We cannot even arrive at a satisfactory estimate of the land grazed in any given year or period. The size of leaseholds provides no assistance either, since this was, until the arrival of farmers, a free range. We also know that, depending on the weather, large sections of the country may have been wholly unsuited to grazing.

A study by D. M. Loveridge and Barry Potyondi has estimated the peak number of cattle in the heart of southwestern Saskatchewan in the period 1880–1907 at forty to fifty thousand head within some 124,416,000 acres (50,350,000 ha). Discounting one-third of the land as unfit for grazing at any particular time, this provides a worst-case ratio of one head per 165.8 acres (67.1 ha), suggesting that the range was actually underutilized in that era. Even allowing for the acknowledged imprecision of this calculation, it seems impossible to conclude that overgrazing was a concern in southwestern Saskatchewan as long as the free range existed.

Some scholars believe that a low ratio of cattle to grass was beneficial to the grassland ecosystem. Andrew Goudie, for example, has argued that

Light grazing may increase the productivity of wild pastures. Nibbling, for example, can encourage the vigour and growth of plants, and in some species such as the valuable African grass, *Themeda triandra*, the removal of coarse, dead stems permits succulent sprouts to shoot. Likewise the seeds of some plant species are spread efficiently by being carried in cattle guts, and then placed in favourable seedbeds of dung or trampled into the soil surface. Moreover, the passage of herbage through the gut and out as faeces modifies the nitrogen cycle, so that grazed pastures tend to be richer in nitrogen than ungrazed ones. Also, like fire, grazing can increase species diversity by opening out the community and creating more niches.[5]

While we have no specific evidence from the early ranching era, the escalating demand for grass and the lack of any comment regarding degradation of the range by the ranchers themselves seems to tip the balance in favor of a positive relationship between domestic livestock and range quality during the first two and a half decades, from 1888 to 1907. As social anthropologist John Bennett has suggested, local ranchers expressed no concern about the resilience of the range until it was fenced, which confined cattle to smaller areas, produced greater stress on the grass, and sparked the first tentative steps toward range management.

Once homesteading began in 1908, the lives of local ranchers were fraught with uncertainty. In a few short years, this cattleman's paradise turned quickly into a hellish range limited as never before by barbed-wire fencing—what one stockman called "those death-traps of the range."[6] In 1911 land surveyor C. F. Miles was astounded at the speed with which fencing had been erected:

> We passed only two settlers on our way in the early morning, then travelling through a ranching country encountered fences which appeared to have no end, and met only one man during the day from whom we could enquire about the outlets in these fences.[7]

Ranchers could not control the erection of fences by farmers. Worse still, from their perspective, was the imposition of the herd law compelling them to fence their own cattle in. In just a few years, the open range had become a web of enclosed pastures.

If the situation in southwestern Saskatchewan was anything like that of range elsewhere on the semi-arid plains in this period, one effect of such enclosure was increased grazing pressure on the native grassland. This affected, in turn, the composition of the range. Unable to move freely as the quantity and quality of pasture diminished in one area, livestock crop the grass beyond its capacity to recover quickly and thus affect the proportion of species. Normally, short- and mid-grasses such as blue grama, speargrass, wheatgrass, and Junegrass constitute most of the vegetation in a short-grass prairie setting like this. Blue grama grass may account for one-quarter to two-thirds of the grass coverage. As ranchers place more cattle on the range, the proportion of blue grama increases noticeably. Once some grasses are eliminated, weeds take their place. Being less palatable to livestock, the weeds flourish and produce seeds in quantities that may soon overwhelm the range. This impact was worsened in the southwest by the high number of horses, noted for their close grazing.

Once the drought of 1918–22 began, permanent degradation of the range became a serious possibility. According to scientists, this was because

> Persistent heavy grazing decreases the supply of soil moisture by reducing the amount of organic matter and vegetative protection at the soil surface. The rate of infiltration is reduced with the result that more moisture evaporates or runs off. Increased insulation at the unprotected soil surface during the warmest season further adds to evaporative loss. The results have been reduced plant vigour, in terms of both height and density, and changes in floristic composition.[8]

This offers an even greater advantage to drought-resistant blue grama grass to the detriment of other species, and the cycle of weed infiltration continues. The postwar decline in livestock prices made the situation worse, as it prompted many ranchers to keep their stock from market, thus adding further to the pressure on the range.

By 1920 the ranchers knew they were in serious trouble. The need to import winter feed and to ship livestock to greener pastures elsewhere in the West were symptoms of the drastic change that had befallen the range. While we do not know precisely when this situation turned into a crisis locally, one study of grass yields at Swift Current found that between 1888 and 1960, the growth of the range exceeded livestock requirements in only twenty-two of the seventy-three years. Furthermore, in twenty-seven of those years, grass stocks were insufficient to meet the demand of cattle on the range.[9] This, with the uncertainty of tenure that characterized ranches in the south country at the same time, forced many ranches out of business.

The remaining ranchers campaigned for development of a federal policy on the management of rangeland and the conservation of grazing resources. They received the assurance that the government would extend grazing leases to a term of twenty-one years and establish a range experimental station to develop strategies for the management of the short-grass prairies of southeastern Alberta and southwestern Saskatchewan. The latter occurred in 1927 with formation of the Dominion Range Experimental Station at Manyberries, Alberta. Consisting of some 18,000 acres (7284 ha), the station encompassed typical native grassland that had never been cultivated, and became the center of short-grass prairie studies in Canada.

The Scourge of Fire

Ranchers, who depended on the ability of their livestock to convert prairie grass into meat, were extremely concerned with the annual devastation from grass fires. Indeed, the impact of fires was so severe that residents of the south country sometimes called them the chief impediment to prosperity.

The government of the North-West Territories had been quick to recognize the threat that fire posed to the commercial progress of the ranchers. In 1879 a system of penalties was introduced that gave careless settlers or travelers the option of a hundred-dollar fine or three months in jail for starting fires not required "for purposes of camp, domestic need, or as a fireguard, or for clearing lands, in the months of December, January, February, March or April."[10] We cannot know whether the threat of such penalties influenced behavior, but clearly not even the rule of law could stop the lightning fires that were exceedingly common. The situation grew even more acute once the main line of the Canadian Pacific Railway passed through Saskatchewan. It then became common for Mounted Police reports to note, as one did in November of 1888, that

> The whole district, with the exception of Wood Mountain itself, was burnt over by prairie fires, which came down from the neighbourhood of the Canadian Pacific Railway. None of these were preventable, nor could their actual origin be ascertained, as they covered such a large area. . . . There will, consequently, be no feed for horses along the line of patrol until well into June of next year.[11]

Because train smokestacks cause sparks, the railway began a policy of burning the grass along its right-of-way for two to three hundred feet (60–90 m) on either side of the tracks. In an extremely dry year like 1893 even this did not help, while in a wet year, such as 1891, it was unnecessary.

The Mounted Police, whose regular patrols allowed them to monitor prairie fires closely, often found themselves in the role of firefighters. When a severe fire fanned by high winds swept through the south in 1894, Mounted Police from Wood Mountain fought it night and day for nine days, but without success. This was but one fire in a dry season that assumed mythical proportions on the plains. John Macoun, traversing this country during the late spring of 1894, before the season's fires commenced, saw a parched landscape whose uplands were all black from the conflagrations of 1893. William Pearce of the Dominion Lands Branch said that there was more destruction from prairie fires in 1894 than in any previous year and

> The time has come when one begins to realize that very drastic measures are becoming absolutely necessary in order to prevent the extensive ranges from being burned off, thus materially reducing their grazing capacity to the great detriment of stockmen who, to a great extent, depend on these ranges for their winter feed.[12]

The percipient Pearce cut to the essence: fires reduced income. In a futile gesture that could not have satisfied many ranchers, the Council of the North-West Territories offered a large prize for the most practical way to make fireguards effective.

As long as the south country remained a ranching enclave, fires continued occur every year. In 1902 alone, fifty fires were reported. One of the worst of the season worked its way north from the Great Northern rail line in Montana and stopped near Wood Mountain. Later in the year, John E. Morgan, manager of the American Bloom outfit near Eastend, reported that all the country north of the Canadian Pacific main line had burned as well. Two years later, Mounted Police managed to secure seventy-nine convictions under the Prairie Fire Ordinance, but still the Wood Mountain area suffered tremendously and few ranchers had sufficient pasture left to winter their cattle. In 1909, most of the country between Wood Mountain and the Canadian Pacific main line burned again, causing the deaths of two people and many horses and cattle. Extensive fires were recorded in 1915, 1916, and 1917.

Elsewhere on the plains, notably where farm settlement was already pronounced, the incidence of fires diminished markedly during the same years. This can be attributed to the greater density of settlement that made the plowing of individual fireguards more effective and the fighting of fires easier. The sparsely settled south country, where plows were still rare, was the last section of Saskatchewan to control prairie fires. They remained an integral component of the environment until the Great War years, and clearly distinguished the area from the remainder of the plains.

Predator Control

A new attitude toward natural predators accompanied the introduction of domestic livestock for profit. While wolfers had sought wolf and coyote skins avidly in the preranching era, such harvesting of the animals was based on the prospect of financial gain. William Ogle said unequivocally that when he first came to the Wood Mountain area in 1888, he regularly poisoned coyotes and foxes for the dollar that each skin was worth. In the ranching period, these elements of the natural order were perceived for the first time as a serious threat to the rancher's livelihood. Unaware of, or perhaps indifferent to, the place of wolves, coyotes, bears, foxes, and other carnivorous creatures in the region's ecosystem, ranchers and their surrogates attempted to exterminate them. They based their response to the natural environment almost exclusively on the protection of their capital assets.

The destruction of predators was not unique to the ranching community. Rather, it was a pattern of behavior toward wild carnivores that may be traced back for centuries in Europe and to the colonial period in North America. This attitude was directed at birds such as hawks and eagles no less than at wolves and coyotes. Typically, all such creatures were described as "noxious" or, more simply, "bad." The prevailing attitude was well summed up in the name of a piece of Saskatchewan legislation called "The Useful Birds Act." The initial abundance of wild creatures became their downfall as their subsistence needs appeared to conflict with the economic interests of the newly arrived ranching community.

One of the first direct references to the perceived threat predators posed to the ranching community came in 1894 when the younger Pascal Bonneau informed the North-West Mounted Police at Wood Mountain that either bears or wolves were killing his cattle. This may have been an unusual occurrence at the time, for Bonneau thought that fires in the Milk River country had forced the predators east in their search for food. In 1897 a Willow Bunch stock-raiser reported the loss of one hundred head of stock to "timber wolves or some other species of wild beast."[13] The report brought concerted action by local ranchers, who immediately put up a reward for the head and skin of the responsible predator. In 1898 the territorial government put $1000 at the disposal of the Western Stock Growers Association for the destruction of wolves on the following basis:

bitch wolf over three months old	$7
dog wolf over three months old	$5
wolf pup under three months old	$2[14]

As it turned out, wolves were said to have done little damage to stock in 1899. This series of incidents is none the less telling for that, as it clearly shows that stock-growers saw predators as a problem and, just as important, that government officials heeded those concerns.

By 1907, the Saskatchewan government had appointed wolf bounty inspectors throughout the province, including men stationed at Willow Bunch, Wood Mountain, Swift Current, Gull Lake, Maple Creek, and Eastend. Between 1907 and 1911, the Maple Creek area accounted for the vast majority of kills, suggesting that the species had already been extirpated elsewhere. From the perspective of the ranchers, however, the government response sometimes seemed inadequate or inappropriate. In 1907, for example, Mounted Police attempted to arrest a well-known wolfer from Eastend named Norbert Adams for possession of venison out of season, causing Adams to flee to the United States. This caused great consternation among the ranching community, for they widely thought that Adams afforded local cattle more protection than the entire police force.

The destruction of predators mounted as farm settlement spread across Saskatchewan. While local data are not available beyond 1911, statistics for the province as a whole reveal that the slaughter of wolves peaked as early as 1911 at 270 head and then steadily declined, with only two comparatively minor rises. The first occurred in 1917–18 (59 head) and the second in 1923–24 (31 head). The situation with respect to coyotes was more grim. For one thing, the pattern of extirpation was different, with the annual kill of about 7600 head in 1911 and rising to a staggering 35,794 in 1918–19 before beginning an even more precipitous decline.[15]

In neither case are the factors behind the kill pattern apparent. The size of the bounty did not change significantly in that period; indeed, ranchers south of Swift Current often complained that it was too low and sometimes contributed out of their own pockets to provide a greater financial incentive. In 1913 the provincial government did raise the adult wolf bounty from seven to ten dollars, at a time when agricultural income as a whole was low due to the prewar recession. According to the Department of Agriculture, this made a difference:

> During 1914 they killed an exceptionally large number of coyotes. The open winter and the financial stringency were in a measure responsible for the increase, and the results are most satisfactory.[16]

We must remember, as well, that the data reflect only applications for bounties, so that the total number of animals killed may have been higher.

It seems likely that the existence of the bounty contributed much to the loss of predators. In 1919, the provincial government removed the bounty altogether on mature wolves and coyotes (but not on pups) because it believed the prices paid by private buyers were high enough to provide an incentive. During the years that followed, the number of officially recorded kills dropped dramatically. Because no private data exist, it is not possible to say whether the total number of kills declined after 1919.

Tracing the slaughter of wolves and coyotes is possible only because this was a kill that the provincial government sanctioned. Unrecorded are the concurrent deaths of similar creatures such as the magpie, the long-billed curlew, and the swift fox (historically referred to as the kit or kitt fox). The magpie nearly disappeared from southwestern Saskatchewan between 1902 and 1911 because ranchers and wolfers put out poisoned bait to eliminate coyotes. We know virtually nothing about the curlew's near loss, except that it happened after 1910. L. B. Potter, a member of the Territorial Natural History Society from Eastend, suggested that the "thieving" magpie, which stole eggs from the nests of other birds, was responsible. When Eloise Leighton arrived in the country in 1906, she remembers that swift foxes were not just a common sight, but a nuisance, too, as they had a habit of chewing up any harness they found for its salt content. The boys in the McEwen family, who homesteaded southwest of Wood Mountain in 1910, held contests to see who could snare the most swift foxes and gophers "as both were plentiful in those days."[17] Equating swift foxes with gophers seems almost unbelievable considering their rapid and almost complete disappearance. Yet people like George Smith, who worked on ranches along the Frenchman River and later resided near Mankota, said that the one and only time he saw a swift fox was in 1926, when he was a young boy and his father made a special point of showing him one in a granary near Bracken. In only a decade or so, another once-numerous species had been virtually eliminated.

The Light Touch of the Rancher

American historians have made much of what they saw as a direct relationship between unregulated ranching and impairment of the range on the Great Plains region of the United States. Overgrazing was a fact of life on many western American ranches as early as 1880. Canadian ranchers never faced such a massive calamity and southwestern Saskatchewan seems to have escaped such consequences altogether until about 1920. This is not to say that the industry of ranching did not affect the environment, only that its impact in southwestern Saskatchewan was much less pronounced than elsewhere on the Great Plains in the years 1880 to 1930. Just as the American catastrophe resulted from unbridled capitalism, the local crisis, when it did come, was clearly related to the pursuit of profit at the expense of the environment.

The ranching community was not, of course, the first to link capitalism and a new perception of the environment on the grassland frontier. Both the Métis *hivernants* and the Native Peoples subscribed to the same ethic during the mid- to late nineteenth century. Driven by the quest for profit and the tremendous difference it made to their material lives, they were active participants in reducing the vast herds of plains buffalo to a few stragglers. Once they had depleted this resource, the Native Peoples in particular cut a wider swath of faunal destruction. While this was obviously not done for profit, but rather to avoid starvation, it nonetheless lengthened the chain of ecological impacts. Those Métis and French-Canadians who remained after 1880 increasingly diversified their profit-making endeavors to include whatever opportunities were at hand, including small-scale stock-raising. Once ranching was well established in southwestern Saskatchewan, they, along with incoming ranchers, judged the value of any component of the environment solely in terms of its contribution to a financial bottom line. Thus it was that ranchers considered wolves and prairie fires equally pernicious.

Ranchers were slow to recognize and admit their negative impact on the range, perhaps because it was merely one factor among many influencing the environment by the 1920s. Had they understood the physical connection between drought, overgrazing, and range composition, they might have been even more damning in their condemnation of the dryland farmers who surrounded them after 1908. As it was, no one truly grasped the cumulative effect that their economic pursuits were having on the grasslands environment.

Gathering buffalo chips for fuel was a routine activity in the treeless south country. *Courtesy of Provincial Archives of Manitoba, N11943-Boundary Commission Collection 1872-74.*

An Assiniboine camp near Fort Walsh, 1878. The area was home to as many as seven different Indian tribes in the late 1800s. *Courtesy of Saskatchewan Archives Board, R-A3959.*

The "cleansing" of the buffalo landscape near Gull Lake. Buffalo bones, all that remained of the great herds that used to pass through the area on their annual migrations, are piled up along rail lines for shipment to the East. *Courtesy of Saskatchewan Archives Board, R-B3195.*

The J.A. Gaff Ranch at Battle Creek, 1912. To the first local ranchers, the southwest was a vast, unbroken sea of grass. *Courtesy of Saskatchewan Archives Board, R-A7771-1.*

The Z-X Ranch at Eastend (circa 1914) was among the wave of large-scale American concerns that entered Canada after 1890. *Courtesy of Saskatchewan Archives Board, R-A6811.*

Herds of horses awaiting shipment to eastern markets were a common sight in the south-west after the drought of 1918-22. Aimé Therrien's herd, corralled at Ponteix in 1926, was sold to raise money for the purchase of a tractor. *Courtesy of Saskatchewan Archives Board, R-B11862a.*

Hunting coyotes for provincial bounty money was a common activity between 1905 and about 1920. *Courtesy of Wood Mountain Historical Society.*

The Better Farming Train toured the south country annually, providing local farmers with the most recent advice on how to cope with their semi-arid climate. *Courtesy of Saskatchewan Archives Board, R-A137-10.*

The coveted Gopher Shield, awarded on Gopher Day to the school with the greatest harvest of gopher tails. This shield was won by the Charlotteburg School District No. 1755 in 1917. *Courtesy of Saskatchewan Archives Board, R-A20630.*

Farmers lining up for relief fodder during the drought, circa 1930. *Courtesy of Saskatchewan Archives Board, R-A16397.*

An aerial view of drifting soil near Assiniboia, 1930s. Between 1931 and 1941, 25 percent of the homesteaders who had been lured to this land by the government eager to settle the West had abandoned their farms. *Courtesy of Saskatchewan Archives Board, R-B8255-1.*

THE DRYLAND FARM

FIVE
Into the Crucible

Those who tried to farm the dry lands of southwestern Saskatchewan were among the least fortunate of the tens of thousands of homesteaders who had been sweeping ever more westward across the prairies and parklands of western Canada since the 1880s. While the first settlers occupied the choicest lands and ignored areas that promised only marginal cereal production, those who arrived later had no choice but to accept the poor lands that were left if they wished to farm at all. Many believed the oft-repeated federal government argument that "proven" dryland farming techniques could make their dry homesteads produce bountiful grain crops, while a few, erring on what they thought was the side of caution, heeded the growing volume of advice from both the federal government and, after 1905, the provincial administration of Saskatchewan, that establishing a mixed farm was the path to success in such an inhospitable land. Seldom had trust been so misplaced.

Saskatchewan led the nation in farm settlement in the new century. By 1905–06, the province accounted for two-thirds of all Canadian homestead entries. But increasingly dense settlement soon brought a shortage of high-quality arable lands, pushing incoming settlers closer and closer to the margins of productivity. This voracious appetite for land—of any quality—peaked just as the tragic winter of 1906–07 forced many ranchers out of business. As the influence of the ranching community waned, politicians paid greater heed to the needs and demands of both established and prospective farmers. The result was the amended Dominion Lands legislation of 1908 that increased the potential area available for farming and thereby opened the dry south country to farm settlement.

As a result, the population of southwestern Saskatchewan rose dramatically. In 1906 it held only 46,560 people; a decade later the total was 178,200. In the same period, the number of farms rose from 8750 to some 38,000, embracing nearly 14 million acres (5,665,599 ha), and the area of cropland increased from a little more than 0.5 million acres (202,343 ha) to almost 4.5 million acres (1,821,085 ha). According to one royal commission on agriculture, "The attraction of free land . . . was so strong that when other areas had once been gone over and the best of them homesteaded, no excuses were accepted by those who wanted to file in the Southwest."[1] This was a land rush to equal the best of them.

The regional environment weighed in heavily against these newcomers. Together, climate and poor soil present a major obstacle to the success of grain farming in the southwest. When the environment does cooperate, farmers may produce bumper crops that rival any in the West, but over the longer term the margin for success in monoculture cereal agriculture is slim. To grow and harvest a crop successfully in this, the heart of Palliser's infamous triangle, farmers must await the advantageous conjunction of many circumstances, none of which they can influence. Even if they choose their land with an eye to the most fertile local soils, they must still rely on the rains to come in the spring and stay throughout the early summer months to germinate the seed and bring the vulnerable seedlings to maturity. The temperature must remain moderate, for frost and excessive heat can severely damage immature crops. The winds must not blow too hard, especially when the air is hot, for this desiccates the green shoots. And the unpredictable midsummer hailstorms must rage elsewhere upon the land. In such a region, the possibility of crop failure is considerable.

Although southwestern Saskatchewan is mostly easily tilled plain with an absence of tree cover, it offers a variety of soils. Most are classified as chernozemic. These are the brown soils of the mid-latitude steppes—dark-colored near the surface, brownish below, and underlain by a gray horizon of lime carbonate. Because of high evaporation rates and the small amount and unreliability of precipitation in the region, some of these soils—particularly those of light texture—will not grow cereal grains successfully.

In the Cypress Hills area, soils range from brown to dark brown to black and medium to fine texture. Dark brown soil is fairly productive but locally soils may have poor structure and high salinity, and most—some 73 percent—have a structure that restricts root penetration. The Swift Current area contains mainly glacial till of chernozemic origin. Medium-textured dark brown soils occupy about 15 percent of the district, with brown soils occupying about 72 percent. The rest are best suited to pasture land. To the east, the Wood Mountain district contains mainly medium-textured glacial till of chernozemic origin. Here brown soils cover more than 60 percent of the area, while dark brown soils cover only 6 percent.

The vagaries of climate match those of soil. In July the mean daily temperature reaches 68°F (20°C) over parts of the southwest and southeast and decreases to about 60°F (16°C) in the northeast. Higher elevations interrupt the general pattern of temperature distribution, as illustrated by the Cypress Hills, where the July mean is about 60°F (16°C). Average daily temperatures for January are above 10°F (-12°C) in the southwest (13°F or -11°C at Maple Creek) but fall off rapidly to the northeast. In other words, temperature varies greatly with latitude. The southwest section of the province is also affected by warm, dry chinook winds that sweep eastward across the southern plains of Alberta and interject brief thaws into the normally cold winters. The mean daily temperatures for July and January do not express, however, the great ranges in temperature that afflict the region. During July, most reporting stations in southern Saskatchewan have recorded absolute maximum temperatures of more than 100°F (38°C). In January, the extreme minimum for southern Saskatchewan is about -44°F (-43°C).

One great advantage the south does have over most of the province is its long frost-free period and, therefore, the length of its growing season. Each year, residents of southwestern Saskatchewan enjoy about one hundred days when the temperature remains above 32°F (0°C), fully a third more than their northern provincial neighbors. The only negative aspect of this is that frosts may occur in any month. Light frosts during the spring are less important to cereal and forage crops than they are to more tender garden crops. Nevertheless, frosts in either late spring or early fall may be critical. The related growing season, which is usually defined as the period after the mean daily temperature reaches 42°F (6°C) in the spring to the date it falls below that temperature in the fall, is also longest in southern Saskatchewan at 180 to 195 days.

The beneficial length of the growing season may easily be offset by a lack of precipitation at critical times, for it is not merely a question of how much rain falls but also when it falls. Much of Saskatchewan is classed as semi-arid to sub-humid, with precipitation being least in parts of the southwest. There the annual average is less than twelve inches (30 cm). An increase to eighteen inches (46 cm) or more marks uplands such as the Cypress Hills. Fortunately for agriculture, the south part of the province receives 50 to 70 percent of its precipitation during the growing season (May through September) with much of this falling in June and July. Because of relatively low temperatures during the growing season, the effectiveness of the precipitation is greater than the annual total suggests. Less moisture evaporates from the soil and transpires from plants than would be the case at higher temperatures.

To this rich climatic stew must be added the potential impact of the wind, for the air currents that sweep over southern Saskatchewan are rarely calm. Their direction varies, depending mainly on the movement of pressure systems across the area. Westerly winds are most common, with average velocities ranging from sixteen miles per hour (26 km/hr) in the more southerly reaches to twelve miles per hour (19 km/hr) in the northern sections. The steadiness and strength of the wind influences soil drifting and water evaporation.

Limited water supply worsens the problem of water retention. No large rivers flow through southwestern Saskatchewan. The Frenchman River and other small streams, such as Battle Creek, flow from the Cypress Hills into the Milk River drainage basin in Montana. More common are streams that flow into enclosed basins. Some of these form large, shallow saline lakes such as Big Muddy and Old Wives. Intermittent streams feed the lakes and thousands of small ponds. All are essentially evaporation basins, losing their water to the atmosphere so that only those with strong groundwater recharges survive the summer.

As if environmental uncertainty were not a sufficient impediment, grassland homesteaders faced the additional obstacle of a poorly developed transportation system. This was the case though they settled the area during the greatest period of railway competition Canada has ever known. The major railway companies of the day—Canadian Pacific, Canadian Northern, and the Grand Trunk Pacific—shared none of the federal government's optimism about the agricultural prospects of southwestern Saskatchewan. As such, homesteaders were hobbled for years—decades in some cases—by their inability to move grain to market.

This was not what incoming settlers had expected. When the land office for the south country opened at Moose Jaw in 1907, for example, the ensuing rush for homesteaders was based on the prospect of a railway connection to the main line in the immediate future. As one contemporary report indicated:

> A large portion of this district, lying to the south and south-west of Moosejaw [sic], is not yet surveyed. That this section of the country is very promising from an agricultural point of view, will be observed from the fact that of the large number of townships which were surveyed and opened for homestead entry last season, very few of these homesteads are now available for entry, while squatters are going into residence in adjoining townships, in advance of survey. Other parts of the district are receiving similar attention, and as most of these newly settled districts are many miles from railroads, the settlers are anxiously awaiting the advent of railway communication.[2]

It was 1913, however, before a Canadian Pacific branch line extended across the southern plains from Weyburn to Lethbridge via Assiniboia. Repeating a pattern nearly a century old, the line skirted the driest parts of the region altogether, clinging instead to its northern periphery.

Farmers elsewhere in the district continued to make long journeys to move their grain to market. Nick Coroluik of the Flintoft district, for example, would spend four days on the trail taking wheat to the elevator in Moose Jaw. George Caragata lamented the fourteen-hour haul he made regularly from Wood Mountain to Limerick between 1914 and 1927. Hauls of forty to fifty miles (65–80 km) were typical. Worse yet, most farmers could haul no more than a hundred bushels at a time in tank or tandem box wagons. As historical geographer P. L. McCormick has pointed out, transporting grain by wagon a distance of more than ten miles (16 km) was simply not economical and discriminated against the small farmer.

Sometimes, the lack of branch lines discouraged farmers from growing wheat altogether. Near Willow Bunch, for example, it was reported that "little grain is sown owing to the long distance from a railway."[3] Land surveyor G. C. Cowper found the same situation at Wood Mountain where "on account of the rough nature of the country and the long haul to the railroad, little grain is grown."[4] Testifying before the Royal Commission on Immigration and Settlement in 1930, Al Smith, a twenty-nine-year veteran of the southwest, summed up the sentiments of many with his statement that "the distance from railroads was what handicapped this district and slowed up development."[5]

Better railway connections were slow in coming, particularly after the financial crisis of the Great War brought branch line construction to a halt throughout western Canada. The efforts of local lobby groups such as the Southwestern Saskatchewan Railway Association were in vain. Not until the mid- to late 1920s did the country south of the Weyburn-Lethbridge line receive service. Between 1923 and 1928 the rails extended to Val Marie, Mankota, Willow Bunch, Wood Mountain, and Rockglen. Even at that, getting to the elevator remained a bone-jarring experience due to the poor quality of the roads.

Roads were another area where investment decreased markedly from north to south. North and west of Wood Mountain, for example, good graded roads were common as early as 1918. Closer to the border, however, there were only rough trails. Some pioneers called them "two ruts" rather than dignify them with the name roads. Richard Greenlay of the Climax district recalled that his father had "a lot of trouble keeping us [children] in buggies because the roads were too rough."[6] Roads remained rough until the 1930s, when many roads were graded for the first time as relief projects.

Awareness of the many impediments to their commercial success lay in the future for most of the immigrants who flocked to southwestern Saskatchewan after 1907. They knew only that Canada's immigrant policies were liberal, its settlement pamphlets alluring, and the costs of establishing a homestead manageable. There were probably many who, like Philip Minifie, a settler on the old "Turkey Track," feared losing out completely if they did not stake a claim to a homestead quickly. Romanians and French-Canadians were attracted by the proximity of their compatriots. Some settlers, like James Frazer, were enticed by the paid agent of a rancher who offered the agent $100 a head to "locate people on other rancher's holdings"[7] after the Dominion government opened the country to homesteading in 1908. Others seem to have been directed to the area by land agents at Regina or Moose Jaw. As many pioneer memoirs suggest, the newcomers began their homesteads in officially sanctioned ignorance and discovered too late that they had been sadly ill advised.

The Technological Advantage

From a technological and scientific point of view, these latecomers to the Canadian plains were well positioned to bring about the ecological transformation of their choice. They were the beneficiaries of nearly thirty years of practical experimentation with dryland farming in Canada and even more in the United States. The trouble was that little of this knowledge was applicable to the extreme conditions offered by southwestern Saskatchewan.

As early as 1886 the eclectic William Saunders, who had been a druggist, a founder of the Entomological Society of Canada, and a fruit importer and breeder, had been retained by the Dominion government to make recommendations about the establishment of a national network of agricultural research stations. Their mandate would be to investigate and determine the best ways to prosper from Canada's special farming conditions. Within less than a year Parliament approved Saunders's scheme and by 1889 research stations were in place throughout the country, a signal tribute to the importance then put on the role of agriculture in the national economy. The first western Canadian station at Indian Head, Saskatchewan, about one hundred miles (166 km) east of Regina, was run by forty-eight-year-old superintendent Angus MacKay, himself a farmer's son and a practical farmer. MacKay's station, like the others, answered to the Central Experimental Farm in Ottawa, where Saunders served as director. This centralized system of experimental stations and substations conducted scientific trials with new grain varieties, machinery, and farming methods to give incoming settlers every chance to succeed in the semi-arid West.

By 1900, MacKay's Indian Head station had assembled a significant body of experimental data on ways to cope with the peculiar climatic

conditions of the western prairies. The principal advances involved land breaking, seed selection, tillage improvement, and weed and smut control. The
station was also an ardent proponent of increased mechanization. In this
Angus MacKay was joined wholeheartedly by officials of Saskatchewan's
Department of Agriculture after its formation in 1905. In fact, the first
report of Saskatchewan's deputy minister of agriculture emphasized the
compilation of detailed provincial farm statistics and reports as to the best
way of satisfying the tremendous public hunger for reliable information.
Accurate and detailed record-keeping would not merely chart the new province's agricultural progress, which was important politically, but would
provide a sound means of spotting trends, identifying concerns, and finding solutions. This was an important step in establishing a strong provincial economy. Departmental officials believed fervently that public
education, combined with the collection, analysis, and distribution of farm
data, would do much to advance provincial growth.

Breaking the sod and preparing a proper seedbed were matters of great
concern in developing the semi-arid areas of the West. By 1909, when
settlement of the dry south country began in earnest, scientists such as
MacKay espoused shallow plowing of the land before the early summer
rains, followed by a second plowing in August or September once the sod
had rotted substantially. Backsetting, as this technique was known, threw
up some three inches (8 cm) of new soil on top of the sod. The farmer
would then harrow the topsoil to create a "fine and firm" seedbed ready to
be sown the following spring. Soil scientists readily admitted, however,
that most new settlers were impatient with this method as it produced less
broken land than the customary spring plowing followed by fall discing
and spring planting. While both techniques produced bountiful crops in
the next year, only backsetting ensured a second good crop because it
increased the soil's capacity to retain moisture. Here, then, was the kind of
challenge faced repeatedly by western Canada's early agronomists: how to
convince homesteaders that their long-term success mattered more than
their immediate results.

Government officials also placed considerable emphasis on the importance of summer fallowing to ensure adequate moisture for crop production. This was not the original intention of summer fallowing. Angus
MacKay had pioneered the procedure in the mid-1880s as a means to eradicate weeds and enrich the soil. Gradually he came to appreciate its other
major benefit, and by the early years of the twentieth century, he invariably identified moisture retention as the main reason to summer fallow.

There seems no doubt that this first generation of farmers heeded the
advice of the government's agricultural experts. In the words of the 1920
Royal Commission on Farming Conditions:

The "summerfallow" method of using the precipitation of three years to grow crops two years, or of two years to grow one crop, has made possible the growing of grain in areas in which it is doubtful whether any other system of tillage and cropping would have produced equally good results. To "summerfallow" has meant to plow the land late in May or early in June and keep it free from vegetation during the remainder of the year so that what rain falls on it is absorbed by it and a considerable portion retained as a surplus for the next year's crop. Some variations have been introduced to meet local conditions, but the foregoing still describes the approved method as generally practised.[8]

Summer fallowing, which proved a panacea in bringing the south country into production, lost its luster as serious drought struck the region between 1918 and 1922. The problem was that the farming implements in use pulverized the soil, leaving it highly susceptible to drifting from the high winds that prevailed in the region. With little moisture to hold the soil together, drifting became pronounced if fields were left without crop cover for an extended period. Members of the 1920 Royal Commission on Farming Conditions, who had no deep understanding of local soil types because little scientific data existed at the time, nonetheless surmised correctly that a natural lack of organic fiber increased the likelihood of drifting. "Soil drifting," they said, "is one of the most serious conditions in connection with grain growing on the lighter soils of Saskatchewan and calls for immediate action."[9]

The commissioners did not know how right they were, for the most important change that grassland farmers wrought in replacing native grass with cereal crops was not even visible. It occurred beneath their newly turned soil, at the level of the chemical reaction. We now know that, comparatively speaking, the thinner and drier soils of the grasslands are less rich in the essential nutrients of carbon and nitrogen than those of cooler or moister climates. Once such soil is cultivated intensively, the amount of organic material declines sharply for the first few years. It then declines less markedly (but still declines) depending on the type of cultivation. Crop rotation can slow the loss but decline remains inevitable unless the nutrients are replaced by chemical means such as regular fertilizing. A study of chernozemic soils in Saskatchewan by Y. A. Martel and E. A. Paul in the mid-1970s found that over a sixty-year period of cultivation, the amount of soil carbon dropped by 33 to 52 percent.

Loss of organic material leads to deterioration of what scientists call the crumb structure of the soil, particularly in clay or silt. A soil with good crumb structure is easily penetrated by plant roots, holds moisture well, and possesses abundant nutrients. In the top six inches (15 cm) of virgin soil, 80 to 100 percent of the minerals are tied up in crumb aggregates. Continuous cultivation typically reduces this proportion to less than 5 percent. One result may be greater compaction of the soil particles, which reduces the soil's ability to absorb moisture. Increased surface runoff then occurs. Very fine soils can also form crusts under the beating action of rain and essentially seal themselves against water penetration. Where strong winds blow regularly, the potential for wind-based erosion during a dry season increases as well. In addition to the problem of soil loss, fine, wind-borne particles can literally shear an emerging crop to the ground.

The link to cereal production is clear. According to C. H. Anderson, an authority on western soil erosion, "Soil drifting started on the prairies as soon as the soils were cultivated."[10] Because drifting was more severe in times of low precipitation, soil scientists recommended the practice of summer fallowing to conserve soil moisture. Without adequate knowledge about tillage practices, however, farmers who summer fallowed as prescribed actually worsened the problem by pulverizing the soil to the point where it drifted even more easily. By 1920 John Bracken of the Manitoba Agricultural College began to argue that

Fallowing is more responsible for soil drifting than anything else. It is also intensified by too much surface tillage, such as discing and harrowing and our people are now giving up these practices on the fallow. It is either harrowed and packed or left untilled.[11]

While this belated grasp of the problem was better than none at all, it came too late to be of benefit to the farmers of the southwest who watched helplessly as their livelihood blew away in the drought-stricken years of 1918–22.

Drought was nothing new in the south country. A 1955 study in Bismarck, North Dakota, a less arid region, shows that between 1851 and 1905 there were twenty-three dry years, twenty-four wet years, and eight years of average rainfall. More recent studies of the Great Plains region have established that the drought cycle is about twenty to twenty-two years.[12] While such studies reveal nothing about the critical distribution of precipitation throughout the year, they nevertheless suggest that conditions may be unfavorable to cereal crop production about one year in three. The earliest grassland settlers narrowly escaped the desiccating July winds of 1907 that shelled grain on the stalk, only to experience pronounced drought late in the summer of 1908. C. F. Miles, who found the bed of the Frenchman River dry as a bone in August of that year, spoke with a seventeen-year veteran of the country who could not recall a drier year. In 1911, a dry spring proved so discouraging to many newcomers that they seriously considered abandoning their homesteads; 1914 was so dry that waterfowl vanished from the area, grain crops yielded only two to ten bushels per acre (per 0.4 ha), and the hay crop was so meager that not even high prices could dampen the demand for baled hay.

Drought

The drought of 1918–22 was different only in that it lasted so long and exacted a much greater human toll. Insufficient moisture year after year meant progressively less precipitation was stored in the soil to sustain the next year's crop. By 1919, southwestern settlers were literally farming dust. The few exceptions to this were those who invested in small-scale irrigation. As early as 1917, surveyor G. C. Cowper reported that some settlers were operating small irrigation schemes on tributaries of the Frenchman. Specific examples are hard to come by, but Ed McPherson, who homesteaded south of Fir Mountain, ran irrigation ditches off Horse Creek in these years. Such ditches were not used to water fields of grain, however, but rather to grow tame hay for livestock feed.

To add to their troubles, local farmers had to cope with other environmental problems. Chief among these was untimely frost, which occurred in 1916 and again in 1918, severe outbreaks of a plant disease known as rust in 1916 and 1922, and devastating hailstorms in 1916 and in 1921. Then in 1919 grasshoppers menaced the crops for the first time in recent memory. The infestation was so severe that the insects remained a threat to crops for at least the next four years.

This series of misfortunes was even more tragic because grain prices were higher than ever. The demands of the Great War forced the average annual price of wheat, which was the main crop in southwestern Saskatchewan, to move from $1.28 per bushel (basis No. 1 Northern) in 1915 to a peak of $2.24 in 1918 before starting to decline. Farmers were, therefore, unable to benefit from the unprecedented demand. Instead, many were reduced to penury. The provincial government helped by guaranteeing mortgage companies the value of funds advanced for seed grain purchases, by arranging free shipment of livestock feed and haying equipment into the drought area, and by providing relief work to those who were destitute.

Without detailed analysis of local land records, we will never know the exact extent of the economic devastation that afflicted farmers in southwestern Saskatchewan before 1930. One study of a "typical" farming township in the Maple Creek area, however, showed that 28 percent of the original homesteaders left permanently in the decade between 1910 and 1920, while an additional 34 percent departed between 1920 and 1930. Altogether, then, about 62 percent of homesteaders in this area abandoned their land between 1910 and the Great Depression.[13] Land surveyor C. F. Miles believed that

> The country along the international boundary [is] fit only for horse and cattle ranching; nevertheless homesteaders crowd in there, break up the land and then abandon it as being too dry. After the land is broken up it is fit for nothing, the native nutritious grasses being exterminated and a rank growth of weed taking their place.[14]

Given increasing knowledge of the environmental limitations of the southwest, the repeated government warnings about the need for diversification, and the difficulties encountered in moving grain to market, how can we explain the headlong plunge of so many farmers into insolvency between 1918 and 1922? The answer lies in a combination of disappointing homesteading experiences, poor business sense, and the strength of wartime demand for agricultural commodities. In southwestern Saskatchewan, as throughout the arable lands of western Canada, the war encouraged agricultural development based on cereal monoculture. The problem was that farmers in the south country had greater need of a hedge against drought than their counterparts elsewhere on the prairies.

When the Great War began in August of 1914, farmers in southwestern Saskatchewan were at the end of a hot dry summer that had ruined their crops. The mild winter of 1913–14 produced little precipitation from snowmelt and the vital spring rains that usually came in May were one-tenth to one-quarter the customary amount. It was so dry that seed failed to germinate. Although June brought frequent showers, much of the damage to the crop was irreversible by that time. Further damage came from the especially hot winds that blew in July when temperatures at Swift Current hovered around 100°F (38°C) for days on end. In August, any remaining grain was wiped out, first by the continuing heat wave and then by severe frosts. The southwest produced wheat yields of 2 bushels per acre, oat yields of 1 bushel per acre, barley yields of 0.8 bushels per acre, and flax yields of 1 bushel per acre. Forage crops and hay fields were similarly devastated, leading many farmers to dispose of their livestock.

Soon, many farmers were unable to meet their financial obligations. Rather than permitting bankruptcy through inaction, the provincial Department of Agriculture assumed the role of mediator between farmers and their creditors. While precise data on negotiated settlements or repayment schemes are not available, it is revealing that the department wrote some seven thousand letters dealing with farm credit matters in the last three months of 1914 alone. Departmental officials were harsh about the inexperience of some farmers. One official wrote:

Many farmers lack a real grasp of the business end of their operations. In some instances we have found that a debtor has paid some creditors in full, leaving nothing to pay other creditors with. It cannot be too strongly emphasized that taxes and mortgage interest should rank with wages and threshing expenses, and the remaining creditors should be treated on a pro rata basis. If our farmers will stand firm in the face of pressure from special collectors and disburse their income from crop and other sources systematically, before long their creditors will realise that the farmer who pays his debts pro rata to the best of his ability, is a reliable person to do business with.[15]

Others did not even try to negotiate with their creditors, preferring instead to apply for government relief. The department was convinced that many farmers could have resolved their difficulties through their own efforts, and it urged that courses in basic bookkeeping be provided to all farmers as soon as possible.

The federal government alone spent more than $8 million to finance the purchase of fodder, feed, and seed grain in the southwest following the 1914 calamity. On one level, this was money well spent, for the wartime demands of Great Britain were extraordinarily high. Prairie farmers had both the means and the incentive to seed heavily in the spring of 1915. If they required further impetus, they found it in skyrocketing wheat prices. In the West as a whole, farm acreage more than doubled between 1911 and 1921, with the amount of improved land rising 95.3 percent. The pattern was the same in the Assiniboia census district, which took in southwestern Saskatchewan. In 1916, the greatest proportion of farm investment was in land, followed by horses, buildings, implements, and labor costs. The weather also cooperated. Southwestern Saskatchewan enjoyed the most favorable crop year in memory, and most farmers harvested a record crop. The principal crops were Marquis and Red Fife wheat that, in some southern districts, produced more than forty bushels to the acre (0.4 ha). The one disheartening event was the prevalence of serious prairie fires south of Shaunavon and Kincaid, and in the Lac Pelletier district, which destroyed many acres of ripening grain.

The negative side to the war years was a tremendous rise in inflation and the cost of borrowing. The price of land, machinery, and labor rose markedly, as did the cost of feed for the many draft horses still in use. Lacking the resources to pay directly for their purchases, farmers borrowed from banks at steadily rising rates or, worse, from implement companies that charged still higher rates. The profit they earned from better yields and high grain prices was typically invested in land and the equipment required to farm it efficiently. The result was not merely creation of a mountain of debt that proved more of a burden than most farmers in the southwest could bear, but also an insufficient degree of economic diversification that would be crippling to many during the extended drought of 1918–22.

"Impossible Surroundings"

Some officials in the Saskatchewan government sensed the makings of a deeper tragedy in the devastation that overtook the south country between 1918 and 1922. Even as F. H. Auld, the deputy minister of agriculture for Saskatchewan, authorized essential relief to the destitute on compassionate grounds, he acknowledged that the assistance would serve occasionally as "the means of continuing in impossible surroundings some [farmers] who cannot be expected to succeed in their present locations."[16] This was a classic illustration of the important difference between those who set government policy and the actions of those in the field who were responsible for implementing the policies; the former tended to do what was politically expedient, while the latter worked hard to make the best of policies that were not always the wisest.

Auld recognized two important facts: that large areas of the south country should never have been opened to homesteading by the Dominion government and that many farmers from that area had failed to heed advice both provincial and federal experts on dryland farming had offered them repeatedly. The former conclusion would have surprised few people; the handful of people familiar with the environment of the southwest realized only too well that the 1908 changes to the homestead regulations were nothing more than political expediency. The latter, however, remained something of a mystery, for the educational campaign for mixed farming in the south had been waged strongly and without interruption from the beginning of settlement.

"Example is better than precept" was the watchword of both the provincial and federal administrations in matters of agricultural education.[17] As centralized bureaucracies with limited staff and budgets at their disposal, they adopted provincewide campaigns to give farmers the best available knowledge on farming techniques. Initially, Saskatchewan did its proselytizing by providing able livestock judges to all agricultural societies who wanted them, by offering grants for seed fairs whose goal was to advertise and distribute good seed grain, and by providing both grants and competent judges for grain field competitions. It was a subtle and cost-effective approach that placed the onus at the local level where many people believed it belonged. To the extent this approach achieved its goals—a difficult matter to assess—it did so because of the proliferation of agricultural societies in Saskatchewan. Forty-four existed in 1898 and the number rose steadily as the years went on. They formed the first ones in the south country at Moose Jaw, Maple Creek, and Swift Current, although it is not possible to determine the extent of the farm hinterland that their membership represented. Formation of societies farther south awaited construction of railway branch lines and the towns they spawned. By 1916, six new communities had applied for agricultural society charters and by 1918 fairs and exhibitions were held annually at communities such as Cabri, Admiral, Cadillac, Assiniboia, Shaunavon, Aneroid, and Vanguard.

The work of departmental representatives (both federal and provincial) in lecturing before various farmers' groups complemented this approach. Early each year the province announced its intention to provide speakers on request at any point on a rail line where farmers could provide free meeting space. The farmers also had to advertise the event. The governments extended this invitation to agricultural societies, farmers' institutes, boards of trade, and even to leading individuals in a district. The demand for this service was considerable. In 1908, they presented ninety-seven lectures; in 1909, the number rose to 163, and they expected that farmers would request more in the following year. The topics on which they lectured were varied; among them were means by which grain shippers could protect their interests, the planting of trees, the benefits of mixed farming, methods of soil cultivation, and the benefits of using good seed grain. Attendance at such lectures rose markedly once slide shows were used to complement the spoken word and, in 1913, the provincial department took this a step further by introducing moving pictures.

Increasingly, print materials played a role in the education of the province's farmers. This was particularly the case after 1912, when the federal government passed the Agricultural Aid Act that provided $500,000 for the development and enhancement of farm education in the provinces. In 1913, an additional $10 million was set aside for use by the provinces over a ten-year period. This fund underwrote the cost of the preparing and distributing farm bulletins to Saskatchewan's farmers. Like the lecture series, the bulletins covered many topics, all of them with a practical orientation. Titles prepared or revised in 1913 included "Blackleg in Cattle," "The Need for Cheaper Money for Agricultural Development," "Hints for Flax Growers," "Co-operative Marketing of Livestock," and "Enrollment and Registration of Stallions in Saskatchewan." They also sent out circular letters (12,730 copies on thirty-seven topics in 1913 alone).

The prewar boom in agricultural education received another significant boost when the province underwrote the costs of the Better Farming Train, an expanded version of a mobile exhibit that the Canadian Pacific Railway had operated jointly with prairie governments since 1906. Farmers in southwestern Saskatchewan, and throughout the province, were enthusiastic about the train. Farm women liked it as well, for its organizers ensured that children were cared for while their parents toured the cars and listened to the lecturers. Premier Walter Scott was particularly taken with the farmers' response and recommended the train cross the southwest again in 1915. He even gave thought to the content of the exhibit. He wrote:

> Considering the nature of the south-western portion of the province and the shortage of feed this year, it has been thought best to lay the emphasis on soil tillage, crop production and weed control. These phases of grain farming will be dealt with very thoroughly in the form of demonstrations and discussions by leading authorities on these subjects.[18]

By 1921, the Better Farming Train comprised four livestock cars, a field crop lecture car, a field crop exhibit car, a poultry and dairy lecture car, a machinery exhibition car, a boys and girls' magic lantern car, a household science car, and a nursery car. Its popularity matched only by that of the circus train, the Better Farming Train continued to operate well into the 1920s.

This extension work had one goal: to provide farmers—particularly those in newly settled areas—with the best available advice on proper methods of farming. Much of the information was generic in nature, applying equally to farm operations in all parts of the province. Increasingly, however, the drought-prone southwest was singled out for special attention. This consisted of a serious attempt to convince dryland farmers of the merits of product diversification. The appointment of William R. Motherwell to the position of Saskatchewan's first minister of agriculture in 1905 set the tone for the entire debate.

Motherwell was an ardent proponent of mixed farming. As an early homesteader in east-central Saskatchewan, and a founding member of the Territorial Grain Growers' Association that fought for the rights of farmers, he was all too familiar with the unfavorable conditions that typified the farmer's lot on the prairies. When he became minister of agriculture, Motherwell advocated the adoption of farming techniques that were appropriate to the West's special climatic conditions. He was also instrumental in establishing Saskatchewan's College of Agriculture at Saskatoon. Few western politicians had a better appreciation of the difficulties faced by dryland farmers.

The limited data available on local agricultural production between 1911 and 1916 suggest that mixed farming advocates such as Motherwell had made some progress. Without question, more farmers were investing in mixed operations. Their available capital or loans went into increased land

and equipment purchases, into such commodities as horses, milk cows, and other cattle, and into the buildings needed to house the livestock. According to the department's annual report for 1920:

> Many farmers, who have lived in the comparatively dry area of the southwest, bear evidence that in numerous cases their cattle and hogs carried them over and supplied them with the necessities of life which they could not have secured from any system of grain farming during the past three years.[19]

Yet the destitution that accompanied the serious drought of 1918–22 also suggests either that many people remained unconvinced of their economic vulnerability or that they had simply not diversified quickly or thoroughly enough.

Hard Lessons in a Hard Land

Unlike the ranchers who saw potential in the grassland of western Canada and then petitioned the Dominion government for legislation that would protect their investments, the first generation of farmers in southwestern Saskatchewan were doubly misled by ill-founded political advice and misbegotten federal legislation to try their luck in the harshest of farming environments. It is a litany of blame that a later generation of policy-makers and historians would proclaim time and again.

Despite severe climatic limitations and serious marketing obstacles, the farmers of the southwest persevered in converting grassland to cereal production. Ignoring repeated setbacks from drought, frost, hail, disease, and insect invasions, they wagered that the unprecedented grain prices of their time would coincide with bumper crops often enough to reward them richly. In this, they were no different from hundreds of thousands of farmers living elsewhere in western Canada. But in the marginal country of the southwest, they eventually lost this game of high stakes—and by then they had altered the environment of southwestern Saskatchewan beyond recognition.

SIX

Lessons Taught in Vain

Better Farming by Government Decree

The economic devastation of the south country after 1918 aroused a clamor among farmers for permanent solutions to their problems within a semi-arid environment. A plaintive letter from local farmer W. H. Walker to F. H. Auld summed up both the experience and the resulting frustration of many residents of the south country:

> I have a half section 5½ miles [9 km] N. W. of Aneroid on which I have buildings worth over $5000 but for 4 years it has not paid expenses. During the last two years it has been rented, but the renter has lost money and left the place much worse than when he got it. The land is a chocolate loam and never blew until last May when the summerfallow wheat was swept right out and the oat crop smothered from a neighbor's summerfallow. I have tried to keep my head on the job myself. In 1911 I introduced Durum wheat. It did well and the first year's crop sold for seed. In 1912 it did well until we took it to the elevators & then the trouble began. Last year many settlers under gov't advice tried Durum again and repeated my experience. Corn is out of the question for it is a success on an average of two years in five. If it were a success we could not afford to handle it and the stock required to consume it. Water for stock would be another problem. Labor too high. I have some Alfalfa & Western Rye both of which have burnt out. Rape & other field fodder for pigs failed me.[1]

As Walker's letter and those of others suggest, local farmers were now willing to listen to sound advice about how best to get their lives back on a profitable track. Many were convinced that if their practical knowledge of the land could somehow be wedded to the best available scientific knowledge, the environmental limitations of the south country could be beaten.

To this end, they asked the government to convene a meeting of authorities quickly. This was done largely through the offices of George Spence, member of the Legislative Assembly for the riding of Notukeu. F. H. Auld later described the nature of the participants in this conference:

> Practical farmers who had made good in spite of adverse conditions were invited to come and outline their methods. Leading professional agriculturists from States with climatic conditions somewhat similar to our own, were invited to come and assist us with their knowledge and experience. Expert agriculturists from our own and other adjoining provinces were invited, so that a goodly number of men who had given the subject much thought were present to take part in the discussions and deliberations of this important gathering.[2]

This gathering, which became known as the Better Farming Conference, met at Swift Current in July of 1920. Attending were many authorities on Canadian dryland farming, and several American experts came to share their experiences as well. Conference delegates reached two main conclusions. First, they agreed that it was unacceptable to have to provide relief to farm families in the south country year after year. Second, they decided that a new regime of farm practices had to be identified and implemented so that farming in southwest Saskatchewan could be put on a sound business basis. They identified three main roadblocks to financial self-sufficiency: drifting soils, insufficient grazing land, and inadequate farmer education. Their conclusions reflected the experience of the conference participants. Nearly all who took an active role in defining the new policy were authorities on dryland conditions, regional farmers who had had the resources or the good fortune to survive the drought years, or representatives of the regional business community. In short, all had a personal stake in continuing to farm the region.

There does not seem to have been any public discussion of the wisdom of this strategy. No farmer came forward at the conference to suggest that cereal agriculture was hopeless in the dry south over the long term. That unpopular position was rarely broached publicly. Only representatives of the regional stock growing industry, clearly a minority, felt no compunction about revealing their beliefs. They said, quite flatly, that

> It seems . . . that to substitute for a flourishing industry, which pays to the Government a very substantial revenue, [an] agricultural proposition which has been conclusively proved to be non-productive, would be the height of folly.[3]

Some western newspapers, such as the pro-settler *Manitoba Free Press*, also voiced this concern. As early as September of 1919, it made its position clear in a front-page feature that excoriated the government for its short-sighted land settlement policy:

> The federal government of Canada had never made any attempt to find out whether these lands were suitable [for grain farming] or not. There was no accurate information as to the rainfall over a period of years. The only people who knew anything at first hand about these lands were the ranchers and when they protested that much of the land was fit for range only, they were laughed to scorn, called land hogs, etc.; and the country was thrown open and settlers flocked in.[4]

The *Free Press* went on to castigate those who had for years claimed that the only obstacle to successful farming in the dryland country was the failure of farmers to adopt "proper" methods of cultivation. It pointed out that despite the continuing drought farmers still plowed under the sod and returned Great War veterans demanded that the last two remaining ranches of any scale—the Wallace and the Matador—be thrown open to them for agricultural settlement.

Even some federal officials questioned the 1908 revisions to the Dominion Lands Act. In 1921, W. W. Cory, deputy minister of the Department of the Interior, put it plainly to Premier Martin:

> There is no doubt but that a great deal of land in southern Saskatchewan and southern Alberta is only fit for grazing and should never have been made available for farming. Our experience has proven conclusively that only a precarious existence can be eked out by the average farmer in some of these sections. It is admitted that there are some sections of good agricultural land but . . . most of the land is unfit for ordinary farming and as a result we have yearly been making substantial advances of seed grain, fodder and relief to those who have been rendered destitute through complete loss of crop.[5]

Cory's perspective remained the minority view in federal circles. Most officials clung, at least publicly, to the hope that some form of "extraordinary" farming would work where "ordinary" farming had failed.

The provincial government response was to appoint a royal commission under the chairmanship of W. J. Rutherford, dean of Saskatchewan's agricultural college. It comprised three committees of inquiry: one dealing with drifting soils, a second that looked into the availability of pasture as an essential component of mixed farming operations, and a third that considered extension services. Besides touring the south to gain an accurate picture of conditions, all committee chairmen held community meetings beginning in September of 1920. They then prepared separate reports for the commission. The final report of the commission, integrating the recommendations of all three committees into a broad strategy for addressing the problems of the south country, was presented to the minister in January of 1921.

The Committee on Drifting Soils

The Committee on Drifting Soils identified means of controlling and preventing soil drifting and of reclaiming lands already eroded by wind. Like all of the commission's committees, it was in the hands of some of the best dryland authorities of the day. It had three members: Professor R. Hansen of the College of Agriculture in Saskatoon, provincial Field Crops Commissioner S. H. Vigor of Regina, and Professor Manley Champlin, an agronomist from South Dakota. Besides the public hearings, the main work of the committee members consisted of a detailed investigation of about 150 square miles (40,000 ha) of drifted land around Mortlach and Tessier.

In the main, the committee adopted the views of John Bracken on soil drifting and its prevention. Formerly professor of field husbandry at the University of Saskatchewan, and now with the Manitoba Agricultural College at Winnipeg, Bracken was widely known for his unrivaled grasp of western Canadian dryland conditions. In fact, the committee's principal contribution to the final report of the commission was an extended quotation from Bracken's *Dry Farming in Western Canada*. Bracken's long experience led him to surmise that soil drifting not only hurt growing crops but diminished the quality of the soil itself. Given the newness of soil science as a profession in 1920, this was a remarkable insight. It influenced profoundly the sort of remedial measures that Bracken—and the Committee on Drifting Soils—recommended.

Bracken argued that the three main natural conditions causing soil drifting were finely textured soils, low precipitation, and high winds in summer. Matters worsened considerably when farmers practiced unsuitable tillage methods and failed to return enough organic matter to the soil through crop rotation or by turning under their stubble. In combination, these factors could produce short-term ecological disasters such as those that had afflicted the south country since 1918. They could also cause longer term impairment of the soil's productivity. According to Bracken, farmers had many effective options. These included:

- packing the soil to bring available moisture to just below the surface, where it would serve to bind together the fine soil particles;

- increasing the soil's organic content by growing perennial or biennial hay crops, by applying manure, or by plowing under green crops;
- modifying the structure of the soil by cultivating rough, "cloddy" surface ridges;
- growing protective crops such as grasses, alfalfa, sweet clover or winter rye, or by leaving crop stubble standing over winter, to minimize drifting during winters with little snow cover; and
- planting closely spaced windbreaks (trees, hedges, or fences) to lessen the extent of drifting.

The problem, then, was not a lack of solutions; rather, it was a lack of awareness of known solutions that had resulted, predictably, in a failure to adopt those solutions.

To Bracken's extensive list of ameliorative measures, the committee added the experience of comparable jurisdictions. From Kansas, they received advice to adopt the practice of ridging the soil at right angles to the direction of the prevailing winds. From North Dakota, they learned of the beneficial effect that winter rye crops had on drifting when coupled with a system of limited tillage. From Manitoba, they heard that farmers were spreading manure or straw on cropland to prevent it from drifting or to arrest the movement of soil after drifting began. Committee members did not strongly endorse these practices, which remained experimental, but neither did they shrink from mentioning them as potentially beneficial. One of the committee's most direct and, over the long term most significant, recommendations was for a comprehensive soil survey of Saskatchewan.

The few soil surveys conducted to that time were random and localized. Soil "experts" of the day merely accumulated empirical evidence that gradually became accepted wisdom. Their conclusions were remarkably accurate given their origins, but what was needed was more in-depth knowledge on the specific types of soil in the province, particularly in the unstudied southwest. The committee deemed scientific knowledge essential to rational planning for the economy of the south country.

The Committee on Grazing

While initially it seems odd that grazing should emerge as one of the three central issues before the Better Farming Commission, there were two sound reasons for its inclusion. First, those already engaged in mixed farming had weathered the drought crisis best and represented the view of the dryland area that governments had advocated since 1908.' Second, grazing leases would soon be emerging as a matter of debate as the ten-year leases issued in 1916–17 moved toward expiration and possible renewal. However much ranching's status had been eroded by homesteading since 1908, southwestern Saskatchewan remained the heart of the province's stock-raising industry, with more than two million acres (81,000 ha) under Crown lease south and west of Moose Jaw.

The immediate concern was that homesteaders had enlarged their cereal operations to the point where their small pastures could no longer accommodate their cattle. This was not a problem in the winter, when farmers kept their stock close to home and fed them hay and grain, but in the summer the limited pasture land was unable to support cattle on a sustained basis.

In their efforts to find enough grazing land, some farmers struck barter arrangements with local ranchers to run their small herds on leased land during the summer months in exchange for a calf or other consideration in the fall. These deals were probably commonplace because ranchers, like their farming neighbors, were finding it difficult to earn a profit. The problem, according to the Better Farming Commission, was that land holdings were taxed according to size rather than productive value. With beef prices low, pasture quality low, and grazing lands hard to find, many ranchers in the south were unable to make their fixed costs and taxes. The Dixon brothers of Maple Creek, astute businessmen with deep roots in the region's ranching community, complained that in 1919 and 1920 they had been compelled, at considerable cost to themselves, to ship their livestock to better pastures in Alberta to avoid selling or starving them. Clearly, the existing allocation of lands in the southwest was not serving the needs of either ranchers or farmers.

After reviewing the matter, the committee recommended the establishment of public grazing lands such as those in forest reserves under the authority of the Forestry Branch. The idea was that pasture land would be set aside for common use by anyone who needed seasonal access to grass. Administration of these fenced community pastures, as they became known, would rest with a regional cooperative organization, which would provide range management in exchange for a grazing fee per head of stock. The land would not be tied up because permits would only be issued to a limited number of grazers annually.

As committee members saw it, benefits to such an arrangement included:
- Efficiency: a large area could be fenced at a lower cost per square mile than a small area, and excellent herd supervision could be offered at minimal expense to the individual stock grower.
- Better herd management: the range could easily be subdivided to segregate different classes of cattle (breeding stock, heifers, steers), and even the smallest stock-raiser could have access to top-quality bulls.

- Better range management: range quality could be monitored properly and cattle shifted about as necessary to ensure optimal use of the grass.
- Better marketing: the segregation of cattle by class would enable the pasture cooperative to assemble carloads of uniform stock for shipment and sale, and the branding of all pastured animals would ensure equitable distribution of the proceeds.

This thinking reflected the cooperative principle that had been sweeping western Canada for a decade or more. Everyone saw its extension to grazing as beneficial because it rationalized land use, promised lowered costs, and formalized the cooperative relationship that many ranchers and farmers had already struck.

Community pastures would mean that even if the Crown did not renew ranchers' existing leases, they could remain in the stock-growing business. Inferior croplands would eventually serve an economic purpose as they reverted to the public ownership through abandonment, nonpayment of taxes, or relocation of farmers. Farmers with mixed operations would no longer have to be concerned with the perennial shortage of summer pasture.

To serve these ends, the committee recommended first, that the Department of the Interior give preference to grazing cooperatives when considering renewals of expiring leases; second, that an existing tract of public grazing land in townships 22 and 23 in ranges 13 and 14, and township 24 in ranges 12 and 13, west of the third meridian, be leased as a community pasture; and third, that community pastures be used primarily for cattle rather than horses. This last suggestion was designed specifically to encourage the sort of diversification farm leaders had sought in the southwest for more than a decade.

The Committee on Agricultural Extension

At one point in their final report, the commissioners wrote that "the principal thing needed may be summed up in the words MORE LOCAL KNOWLEDGE."[6] While it was true that farmers could turn, if they wished, to a host of advisory services, the value of the knowledge they received was highly dependent on its scientific reliability. Just as they felt that they needed an intensive soil survey of the southwest, the commissioners also recommended that additional weather reporting stations be set up to chart precipitation and frost conditions. Most important, they recommended significant changes in the centralized organization of government-sponsored agricultural research stations.

The commissioners identified a need for regional substations of the

College of Agriculture at Saskatoon throughout the province, starting in the southwest. Each substation would address the specific concerns of the subregion. In the words of the commissioners,

> [They would] be located with due reference to climatic and soil conditions, and at convenient centres so that they would be accessible, and they should be of sufficient size to permit of a system of balanced farming being carried on in addition to the series of field husbandry experiments which would be their primary object.[7]

The commissioners went so far as to say that they feared economic failure unless farmers were seen as full partners in agricultural experimentation with equal responsibility for the development and implementation of long-term solutions.

These forthright recommendations were closely linked to the commissioners' abiding belief that only diversified farming would succeed in the south country. "The more the risk is divided," they emphasized, "the less heavily the losses will fall in any one season."[8] It was a familiar litany, but in view of the troubles that so many residents of the southwest had experienced recently the commissioners clearly felt it needed repeating. The report of the Commission on Better Farming Practices also made it clear that if the region were to prosper, government, farmers, and ranchers would have to pull together to develop and implement rational land-use policies.

The More Things Change . . .

The provincial and federal governments tried hard to carry out the recommendations of the commission. They altered existing policies, enacted new legislation, provided financing, and offered more and better extension services. As early as 1921, it seemed the Better Farming Conference and the subsequent commission had infused the south country with the new spirit of cooperation and experimentation. For the first time ever, it appeared that enlightened self-interest would prevail in the chronically depressed southwest of the province.

According to F. H. Auld, the most immediate effect was on the type of crops sown. In his annual report for 1921, he reported that

> There is one feature of the [Better Farming] conference that I might mention, namely the indorsation [sic] by practical farmers and experts of the benefits that would follow the more general use of winter rye in that portion of the province. This crop has been advocated by the department for a number of years and last year, as a result largely, we think, of the conference,

the acreage in that particular crop district was increased from 46,909 acres [19,000 ha] to 773,499 [313,000 ha].[9]

Winter rye was considered a hardy crop that could be used as early summer pasture, or as a grain crop, or both. It could also be grown successfully on virtually any type of soil, making it ideal for the variegated lands of the southwest. John Bracken had long applauded its ability to reduce soil drifting as well. If these virtues were not enough, it also seemed to reduce the spread of Russian thistle and other weeds. Several farmers in the Maple Creek and Piapot district along the main line of the Canadian Pacific Railway had proved its practical utility and the Department of Agriculture felt confident in recommending it. To this end, they distributed winter rye extensively as relief seed in the southwest following the poor crop yields of 1921. While confirming data regarding seed relief at the crop district level are lacking, it may be that this distribution had a significant impact on the number of acres devoted to winter rye in the south country in 1921.

Local farmers also seemed to embrace the new philosophy of cooperative grazing. The provincial Agricultural Co-operative Associations Act offered farmers the means to such organization and they formed several cooperatives in 1921. Any farm districts that chose to form such a cooperative could obtain a ten-year lease from the provincial government on compact tracts of non-agricultural land larger than three sections in extent. The federal government facilitated this by amendments to its grazing leasehold policy in 1922. Henceforth, the province would be given first opportunity to renew expiring leases of grazing lands to establish community pastures. The seriousness of its intent was clear in its decision not to renew the 125,000 acre (50,586 ha) lease of the Matador Ranch north of Rush Lake. In 1923 some farmers organized the Hazenmore Co-op Trading Company to buy out the Warren lease, which could accommodate about one thousand head of stock.

Even agricultural extension meetings dealing with matters pertaining to dairy farming met with unprecedented interest. In 1924 the dairy commissioner noted that

A striking feature of dairy meetings throughout the year [1923] has been the keener interest and greater sincerity in the study of dairy problems by the rank and file of the farming population in all parts of the province. The old situation of a few interested questioners with the remainder of the audience present from curiosity or want of other diversion or even to openly scoff at the man who milks cows has passed. Today almost the entire community frequently turns out to dairy meeting[s] and shows a lively interest because they sense the direct connection between a dairy herd and a dependable income.[10]

As was the case with so many other matters, agricultural officials had long advocated the purchase of at least enough milk cows to provide all of a farm family's needs. By 1925, privately owned dairies were operating in Shaunavon, Assiniboia, and Maple Creek.

The governments also made good on their promise to provide more localized agricultural experimentation and extension services. In 1920 the federal government established an experimental station at Swift Current. Its specific mandate was to investigate farm problems related to drought in the southwest. More specifically, its work addressed the issues of soil drifting, weed control in relation to moisture conservation, and the efficient application of labor and machinery. "From the outset," according to the station's historian, "the task was to prove that economic survival was possible in this area of limited moisture."[11]

For its part, the province provided better extension services through the deployment of field representatives in the southwest. There had been extension officers at Shaunavon and Swift Current as early as 1914, but their services were discontinued during the war years. In 1922 the province hired five agricultural graduates to work in the local improvement districts of southern Saskatchewan, centered at Maple Creek, Robsart (two men), Cadillac, and Limerick. They conducted farm censuses in the area, promoted and supervised cooperative experiments with various new crops, investigated crop pests and weed conditions, judged crop and livestock competitions, and directed the local grasshopper campaigns.

To promote greater farm diversification—always the central concern of farm experts—the provincial Department of Agriculture provided significant incentives for the establishment of purebred cattle herds in the southwest. Officials stressed the need for more and better herds of both beef and dairy cattle. The program they enacted enabled farmers to obtain high-quality heifers and breeding bulls at cost. Whenever possible, they obtained these foundation herds from other Saskatchewan breeders. They also emphasized the cooperative element that was possible in this venture: if several farmers wished to pool their cash and share top-quality bulls they would develop the best possible herds in the shortest time.

Cooperation was the common thread in these initiatives. Governments provided the means to ends that all had agreed were critical if farms were to become self-sustaining operations in the south country, and farmers participated with apparent goodwill in the unprecedented opportunities before them. The response of both parties was swift, so swift in fact that, as early as 1923, the director of agricultural extension for Saskatchewan wrote glowingly about a "new spirit of self-help" suffusing the province's agricultural societies.

. . . The More They Remain the Same

Recommitment to farming the south country on this enlightened basis remained strong only as long as the postwar recession lasted. While the governments continued—and even intensified—their research and extension activities in the years that followed, the farming community of the southwest failed to keep pace. Its enthusiasm for the new ethic flagged in lockstep with rising grain prices. Rather than continuing to diversify, farmers rapidly returned to the cereal monoculture agriculture that had been the downfall of so many just years before.

The economic recovery that caused this about-face began in 1924. The mirror image of 1923, which had been characterized by high yields and low prices, 1924 brought low yields and higher prices. These were halcyon days for the western wheat-grower as revolution-wracked Russia was no longer an important grain exporter. Canada, with Australia, the United States, and Argentina, ruled the world grain trade. Increasing demand moved the average wheat price to $1.68 per bushel in 1924, a one-year jump of 61 cents per bushel and the second-best return of the decade. This marked the first upward movement of grain prices since 1920 and, with a concurrent drop in the cost of living, gave considerable encouragement to farmers in the south country.

The same type of roller-coaster ride marked the balance of the decade. A high yield, such as those of 1927 and 1928, might be offset by the prevalence of rust or an unfavorable harvest season that lowered grades. The impact of fluctuations owing to natural causes was cushioned to some extent by the steadiness of wheat prices, especially once the cooperative wheat pools began to handle the marketing of a significant proportion of the western harvest in the mid-1920s. Over the decade, the wheat yields rose in both of the crop districts that encompassed southwestern Saskatchewan. In Crop District No. 3 the average yield was 16.6 bushels per acre (0.4 ha), while that of Crop District No. 4 was 15.7 bushels per acre, not superb returns but much better than the nonexistent yields of 1918–22.[12]

This comparatively favorable decade for dryland farmers brought an intensification of the agricultural trends established between 1908 and 1917. In the decade 1921 to 1931, the number of farmers in eight rural municipalities in southwestern Saskatchewan increased by 6.3 percent. At the same time the size of the average farm holding went from 343 acres (139 ha) to 454 acres (184 ha). In all, an additional 340,000 acres (137,270 ha) of land was "improved," or brought into crop production. Although the number of farm owners declined by nearly 10 percent, the number of owner-tenants rose more than 40 percent, pointing clearly to the fact that they were investing much revenue from farming (or borrowed capital) in land.

The acquisition of more land was compatible with the notion of greater farm diversification but that is not what happened. Data for Crop Districts 3 and 4, although partial, show without question that local investment in cattle, swine, and poultry actually declined over the period 1921–30. The acquisition and improvement of land in the south country proceeded to such a degree during the 1920s that local witnesses before the Royal Commission on Immigration and Settlement in 1930 testified, to a man, that there was little arable land left.

Witnesses before the 1930 Royal Commission on Immigration and Settlement also emphasized that most farmers depended by the late 1920s on mechanized operations (what they called "power farming") and that few engaged in mixed farming beyond their immediate needs. In other words, local devotion to monoculture farming was greater than ever. Statistics for Crop Districts No. 3 and 4 bear this out, showing virtually the same pattern of crop production in the years 1916–30.

Given the experience of 1918–22, it seems odd that most farmers in the south remained unconvinced of the merits of greater economic diversification. They simply did not subscribe to the view, expressed by many government officials, that to engage in mixed farming was to hedge their bets in a tenuous business venture that combined environmental unpredictability with economic uncertainty. Rather, they seemed to believe, as a Grassy Creek Rural Municipality secretary and former banker put it, "that mixed farming is too much work and as long as they can get by with wheat farming they will."[13]

The weight of the historical record to 1930 suggests, in fact, that typically farmers in southwestern Saskatchewan were not husbanders of the soil caring for it an enlightened manner. Rather, they were more like engineers, using the latest science and technology to bend nature to their will, ever conscious that although the natural world might occasionally rebuff their efforts, they were ultimately masters of their own economic destiny.

SEVEN
Making the Environment Anew

The Power of the Plow

As an economic group, farmers conquered the plains swiftly and convincingly. Together they did what many failed to do as individuals: they modified southwestern Saskatchewan's grassland to the point where the presettlement landscape and ecology were scarcely recognizable. Underlain by the latest technology and science, and repeatedly driven ahead by the prospect of quick gain, the farming community showed ingenuity and prowess in transforming the plains into a managed environment.

Unlike ranchers, farmers were not content with the land as they found it for it failed to satisfy their economic imperatives. Apart from some pasture for their small cattle herds and draft horses, homesteaders had little initial use for grassland. Instead, they subscribed to the government view that "the first task of the farmer is to destroy *native* plants in order to prepare a place for *cultivated* plants to grow."[1]

The introduction of exotic grains must rank as the most basic change that farmers brought to southwestern Saskatchewan. Under favorable conditions, these "green immigrants," as one botanist has called them,[2] established themselves quickly, dominating the look of the land and, only somewhat less rapidly, its ecology. Between 1907 and 1914, the total cropped acreage of Crop District No. 3, which included most of southwestern Saskatchewan, rose dramatically from 20,000 acres (8094 ha) to more than 600,000 acres (242,810 ha). Farmers devoted most of this land to wheat production, particularly Marquis and Red Fife, for which there was a buoyant market. Oats, used primarily as horse feed, formed the next largest crop. Barley and flax made up the remainder.

On a romantic level, we can visualize this change as the traditional "sea of grass" being displaced by "waving fields of golden grain." Looking beyond imagery and metaphor, we can also understand the transformation as the outward manifestation of an entirely new economic framework being imposed on the land. That framework derived principally from government legislation that advanced the interests of the farmer at the expense of those of the rancher. Like the notion of a "managed" natural landscape that the federal government was imposing on other western tracts through the creation of national parks, the 1908 revisions to the Dominion Lands Act gave form to prairie settlement enabling farmers of the southwest to replace the softly flowing landscape of untrammeled rangeland vistas with a new landscape marked by square quarter section farmsteads, grid roads that owed little to geography, equally spaced townsites along straight railway rights-of-way, unswerving fence lines, rectangular vegetable gardens, and linear shelterbelts. It was a new landscape reflecting different economic imperatives.

No less than in previous eras, we can "read" the land of the southwest as a historical document. The reduced incidence of prairie fires was one indicator of change. Although train locomotives became more common throughout southwestern Saskatchewan as settlement advanced, the annual number of prairie fires declined steadily until, by about 1917, such conflagrations were rare. The railway companies, dependent as they were on the yields of the cropland that flanked their tracks, could ill afford to set the countryside ablaze. Section gangs routinely set controlled burns of the right-of-way to reduce the likelihood of fire from a cinder-belching steam locomotive. The development of municipal governments and local improvement districts in the prewar years regulated stubble burning for the first time. The construction of roads provided a reasonably effective grid of fireguards that contained any minor blaze that did erupt. And, of course, the sheer density of the population made a significant difference, not only because many settlers regularly plowed fireguards that hindered the progress of a blaze but also because for the first time people were around in sufficient numbers to fight a fire successfully. Besides eliminating the blackened landscape and smoke-laden air of yesteryear, the cessation of annual fires allowed additional trees to take root and flourish in sheltered, well-watered coulees.

A less pronounced impact on the environment came from the settlers' search for heating and cooking fuel. Typically, homesteaders were either too far from the railway or too cash-poor to buy coal from merchants for their everyday needs. At first, they solved their fuel problem by collecting and burning the livestock equivalent of the buffalo chips. By the time of the Great War, however, this fuel was in short supply. Wood was scarce as well. Naturally, demand grew as hundreds of homesteading families put up shelters and fences. Thus, people turned increasingly to local supplies of lignite coal.

The soft, dirty coal known as lignite was found in considerable quantities near Wood Mountain and throughout the badlands along the international boundary. Although of poor quality, it served the purpose when mixed with a small quantity of hard coal that homesteaders might purchase at a settlement. The mines were usually small-scale strip operations. Settlers cleared away the dirt covering the seams and shoveled the coal into wagons by hand. Most often those buying the coal did the shoveling themselves, which helped to reduce their costs. The farmers who owned the mines were able, in turn, to supplement their modest farm incomes with a little ready cash. In 1923, one operator was charging five dollars a load. The proliferation of strip operations suggests the significant degree to which these mines served both purposes. November and December were the preferred months for hauling coal, as the grain harvest was completed and the trails were sufficiently frozen to shoulder the weight of the coal-laden wagons.

On occasion, the coal seam was of sufficient depth and local demand sufficiently high to warrant development of an underground mine. This was the case with the Dawson family mine, on the southwest quarter of section 16, range 1, west of the 4th meridian. The enterprising Dawsons constructed a track on which they pushed (by hand) cars with a capacity of perhaps five hundred pounds (225 kg) each. They needed six to eight carloads to fill one farm wagon. This mine was said to have the added advantage of being situated exactly on the international boundary, so that the owners could dump coal into wagons in either Canada or the United States without paying any duties.

Dual coal and wood operations were rarer still. The Pearson family ran one such operation, called the Six Mile Coal Mine, where they sold not only coal but poplar and willow fence pickets as well. Settlers would come from Lafleche, Gravelbourg, and adjacent districts in such numbers that the Pearsons opened a stopping house to accommodate their customers and to supplement the proceeds from their mining venture.

The demand for coal was great enough throughout the south country that the Sioux, to whom the Canadian government had conceded a reserve at Wood Mountain in 1913, developed an enterprise that apparently lasted some thirty-four years. In 1915 the Department of Indian Affairs learned that the Sioux were mining and selling coal from their reserve lands. Although J. D. MacLean, assistant deputy minister of Indian Affairs, encouraged them in this enterprise, production seems to have been erratic. The remaining records show that they mined 141 tons (128 tonnes) in 1916, 31 (28 tonnes) in 1917, 100 (91 tonnes) in 1920, and 272 (247 tonnes) in 1931.[3]

Just as the prevention of fires and the search for fuel were rooted in economic self-interest, so too were the campaigns of destruction that farmers waged against many species of wildlife indigenous to the area. While they participated in the elimination of coyotes with as much enthusiasm as the ranchers, farmers were alone in their contempt of gophers, which were particularly a problem in the drier areas of the province. Speakers on the farm lecture circuit invariably included this topic in their repertoire. In 1907 T. N. Willing, the provincial weed inspector, addressing a convention of agricultural societies, advised the use of poison bait to keep gopher populations in check. Many farmers had already taken this advice for, as Willing noted, more than three thousand dollars worth of strychnine had been purchased for this purpose in 1907 alone. He was concerned, however, that few farmers knew the proper way of mixing and setting out the bait, so he provided detailed instructions:

> The poisoned wheat should be distributed about the gopher holes about the time the snow goes [in the spring]; and then there is less other food available for the gophers, and one female killed at that time is better than several later in the season. Dissolve 1½ ozs. [50 g] of strychnine sulphate in a quart of hot water, add a quart of molasses and a tablespoon of anise. Heat, mix and pour while hot over a bushel of wheat. Mix and let stand over night, then stir a little fine meal to take up the moisture. A tablespoon at a hole will be enough.[4]

Willing also advised that traps set at the margins of fields would reduce the gopher population considerably throughout the summer months. By 1920, the Department of Agriculture was supplying more than four thousand ounces (125 kg) of strychnine to just six districts.

Good advice and free poison aside, the gopher "problem" persisted. In 1916, the Department of Agriculture enlisted the aid of the schools and declared May 1 to be Gopher Day. This marked the start of an annual campaign of destruction. School children throughout the province were given the day off to roam through local pastures, snaring every gopher they could, for a reward of one cent per tail.

As the Great War continued, and governments everywhere placed increased emphasis on the importance of crop production, the reward for gopher tails increased. In 1919, for example, the six children with the greatest number of tails to their credit each received a Shetland pony, courtesy of grain companies, lumber companies, and the department itself. Runners-up received everything from a pair of registered pigs to baseball outfits to fountain pens. The impact on local fauna was tremendous. In 1920 alone, they destroyed more than two million gophers. The department estimated that one million bushels of grain were likely saved as a result.

Refuge No More

Farmers in the southwest did not engage in direct campaigns of destruction against all local wildlife; some species succumbed indirectly as intense wartime cropping practices destroyed their habitats. Commonly, as with the swift fox, we do not know the precise circumstances of their disappearance, only that they literally vanished from the vast grassland region that had been theirs since at least the time of Lewis and Clark. A 1913 report on the southwest, for example, showed that "big game has almost left this district. There are a few antelope, white tailed deer and black tailed deer. All reports indicate that big game is decreasing in this district."[5] The report went on to discuss the reasons for the decrease:

> The game laws in this district are not observed any too well. One guardian reports: "The provisions of The Game Act are observed somewhat indifferently by farmers in outlying districts, especially in the case of antelope shooting." Elk, deer, antelope and swans are in danger of being exterminated, according to our guardian's reports.[6]

Our main clues about the decline in wildlife populations come from amateurs who conveyed their observations to the province's game guardians. These guardians were few and responsible for immense districts that they covered mainly by rail. In the south country before the 1920s the task of assessing wildlife conditions firsthand was all but impossible.

Game guardian Neil Gilmour, who looked after most of the south country from his base at Moose Jaw, remarked annually on the scarcity of prairie chickens and grouse. He believed that overhunting was one reason for the decline, but he also observed that "farmers when improving their property often unintentionally destroy the natural breeding grounds of the grouse. This is a source of destruction which eventually has an appreciable effect upon the supply of game in certain districts."[7] Gilmour also felt that the devastating prairie fires of the war years significantly affected ground-nesting birds. He further linked their demise to an increase in natural predators that occurred as the price of mink, skunks, weasels, and coyotes dropped precipitously once the Great War began. On the other hand, when the destruction of predators was on the rise, the population of rabbits reached what Gilmour called "plague proportions." There is more than a glimmer of an understanding of what would later be commonly called "the balance of nature" in Gilmour's astute comments, yet he and his counterparts throughout Saskatchewan had few effective means of enforcing the game preservation laws of the day.

Gilmour reserved his most poignant comments for the antelope of the southwest. This timid creature, which may have been more numerous than the buffalo before settlement of the plains, was reduced to as few as fifteen hundred head by 1913. The winter of 1906–07 had been as hard on them as on cattle, but Gilmour mainly attributed the loss to "the encroachment of settlers upon their former breeding grounds."[8] Gilmour became an early advocate of a preserve for antelope, a cause soon championed by his superior, Chief Game Guardian Thomas Willing, and acted upon by the Dominion government after 1915. Eventually the federal government established three reserves, one just south of Maple Creek and the others across the border in Alberta.

Despite the protected status of the antelope, in 1918 Gilmour could find only one remaining herd, near Secretan on the main line of the Canadian Pacific Railway. The seriousness of the situation eventually led the provincial government to undertake its own crude census of antelope in 1922. They estimated that only 250 antelope were left in southwestern Saskatchewan. Eventually, settlers whose lands took in the remaining antelope range began to display a genuine pride in helping to save the species. It would take decades of concerted preservation work, however, before the herds recovered.

"Thieves in the Fields"[9]

It seems that farmers in the south country did not perceive weeds as a menace of the same order as gophers. The provincial government, however, felt differently. The Department of Agriculture designated a provincial weed inspector in 1905 with a mandate to provide sound advice on means of eradication at agricultural exhibitions, stock shows, and similar agrarian gatherings. The premise behind this proselytizing was the same that applied to all of the department's extension work. As the first annual report stated, "All must admit that good farmers cannot be made out of bad by Act of Parliament."[10] In other words, education was key. The weed inspector and, later, his regional subordinates explained that weeds used up the moisture needed by domestic crops. Especially in the drier parts of the province, inadequate weed control affected profits.

Weeds accompanied the agricultural settlement of the south country. As historian Alfred Crosby has pointed out:

> Before the advent of agriculture, there were relatively few of these plants representing any given species; they [weeds] were the "pioneers of secondary successions or colonizers," specializing in the occupation of ground stripped of plants by landslides, floods, fires, and so forth.[11]

The impact of cereal agriculture must be considered all the greater because the native grasses of the Great Plains were among the plant species most resistant to invasion and colonization by non-indigenous forms of vegetation.

Those familiar with the problem in western Canada commonly identified four main sources of weed seeds: animals and birds, water, wind, and people. Animals and birds often distributed weed seeds simply by consuming them and then defecating throughout the country; barbed seeds stuck to their fur or feathers. The construction of railway branch lines into the region brought yet another source of contamination: the oats consumed by the many teams of work horses that pulled the scrapers and supply wagons along the grade. Water, whether in rivers or irrigation ditches, conveyed seeds as well, although this method of transmission was probably not as important in the dry southwest as elsewhere. High winds picked up weed seeds and carried them everywhere, and many were moved about with drifting soil during the years of drought. Finally, most authorities identified the spread of weeds with the spread of settlement.

The authorities often berated immigration officials for their lax inspection of settlers' outfits at the border, holding that many immigrants brought "foul" seed grain with them into the country and initiated an uncontrolled chain of weed infestation. They raised particular concerns about the amount of "dirty" flax seed coming in from the United States. While lax immigration procedures certainly did not help, farmers themselves were singled out as the greatest source of field contamination. In the government's view, farmers frequently used contaminated seed grain, failed to clean weeds off their implements when moving from one field to another, and fed weed-infested feed to their livestock, which then deposited the seeds in all directions.

Saskatchewan's weed inspectors believed that the noxious growth along the province's road allowances resulted from hauling weed-infested grain to market, which spilled out onto the road. They also condemned elevator agents who disposed of their screenings—the weed seeds separated from the grain—by dumping them in low spots on the prairies, thus offering the weeds a well-watered, uncultivated base from which to spread. As ever more exotic cereal grains were imported from overseas, weed infiltration assumed a specific character; according to one authority, some 60 percent of the principal farmland weeds now in Canada are of European origin.

In 1906 the Department of Agriculture expanded its vigilance by hiring fifty-five weed inspectors to serve sixty-one districts throughout the province. Their annual reports document the infiltration and spread of a variety of weed species. In 1905 they reported that the Moose Jaw district had plenty of purple cockle, a tall, flowering plant whose seeds impart a dark color and bad flavor to ground grain and which can, if eaten in sufficient quantities, poison young chickens. A year later, stinkweed and tumbling mustard were particularly bothersome in the southern districts. The mustard problem was attributed to the neglect of weed control along old fireguards, roadsides, and uncropped fields. Entire heads of this plant, each containing as many as 1,500,000 seeds, would break off and roll with the wind, ensuring that it swiftly attained a good foothold in the region. Russian thistle, a globelike plant that snaps off at the root when mature, spread by the same means throughout the south country. It was widely reported as early as 1909.

If the weed inspectors had a particular nemesis, it was wild oats. This weed was associated with cereal agriculture because of its tendency to drop its early-maturing seeds either before or during harvest and to retain its later seeds to be harvested with the grain crop. Cultivation of stubble fields in the fall started germination of the seeds, which could then be destroyed either in the fall or in the spring before they had a chance to produce more seeds, but seed in harvested grain could only be eliminated through thorough cleaning. The reluctance of many farmers to clean their seed grain was said to account for much of the contamination of the south country.

Weed inspectors made much of the inability of newly minted farmers to comprehend the impact of the weed problem. This remained a serious concern of the Department of Agriculture even after 1909 when it devolved day-to-day responsibility for weed control to the rural municipalities. One official estimated that carelessness caused only one-quarter of the weed problem; the rest resulted from indifference.

Recognizing the scope of the problem, the province offered a series of short courses annually to all municipal weed inspectors and defrayed all related costs to encourage participation. Yet when Neil Gilmour attempted to arrange a meeting of municipal inspectors from the south in 1912, only two of the six attended. To this indifference was added the problem of abandoned land along the international boundary. As C. F. Miles reported in 1911, when settlers broke the land, destroyed the native vegetation, and then gave up because no grain would grow successfully, the infestation of weeds that followed was rank in the extreme.

In 1914 those trying to prevent the spread of weeds in the south met yet another obstacle. The drought produced short crops and small incomes, meaning that the region's municipalities had fewer tax dollars with which to prosecute the war on weeds. According to Gilmour:

What money they had was used for road building and other improvements. It was not easy to persuade their men, that all-important as were these improvements, the same money thoughtfully and wisely spent in using the means provided for cleaning up the comparatively few dirty farms and in guarding against the introduction of weeds from outside, would have produced in the future dividends immeasurably greater.[12]

The government believed, in fact, that many farmers took advantage of the absence of municipal weed inspectors. This was particularly true during the drought of 1918–22. Matters merely worsened when the grasshopper infestation caused a diversion of funds from the provincial weed campaign.

Control of weeds depended most on the willingness of farmers to eradicate them. Until the 1930s, when herbicides became more generally available, the vigilance of individuals remained the best weapon against weeds. As the provincial Department of Agriculture never tired of saying, it was merely a question of following good farming practices. The failure of many to adopt those methods before 1930 changed forever the vegetation of the grasslands. There were all too many instances where weeds had, as Dominion weed experts noted first in 1909, "taken possession of the land."[13]

Plant Diseases and Insect Pests

The endless fields of grain that came to characterize the whole of the North American Great Plains in this century proved equally fertile ground for plant diseases and voracious insects. These natural perils got their start on the winter wheat crops of the Texas plains and then worked their way north as the season advanced. Monoculture agriculture encouraged their spread by providing the same favorable conditions year after year.

Stem rust and stinking smut were the most common plant diseases affecting local cereal crops. Rust, a fungal disease, takes its name from the brick-red pustules that appear on stems or leaves in the summer months. Each pustule contains hundreds of thousands of spores that are easily carried on the wind to infect other plants. Until 1917, one year after a very serious outbreak, no scientific work had ever been done on rust. Eventually, rust-resistant types of wheat would prove the best means of alleviating its spread.

The crop losses caused by stinking smut were second only to those of rust. The heads of smutty wheat, as it is known, have a bluish-green tinge. The disease prevents proper development of the kernels and renders sound grain unsuitable for milling. Angus MacKay had long encouraged farmers to treat their seed grain with a bluestone solution (copper sulfate) before seeding to reduce the incidence of smut, but the campaign was far from successful. As early as 1906, the provincial Department of Agriculture recommended that farmers treat their seed with either bluestone or formalin (40 percent formaldehyde), but officials were less than pleased with the lack of attention that many farmers gave to the problem.

Until better means of control were found in the 1930s, rust and smut wreaked havoc with the prairie economy. One estimate placed the loss of Saskatchewan and Manitoba wheat crops to rust for the years 1925–32 at more than $35 million. Losses attributable to smut were smaller but still substantial, roughly $12 million for Canada as a whole in the years 1920–23.

Newly broken or repeatedly sown cropland also encouraged the spread of insects such as wireworms, cutworms, and sawflies. Wireworms, the larval stage of the click beetle, were of particular concern in grassland regions or where the sod had been broken recently. The only remedies available to farmers before the development of commercial pesticides in the 1930s were the setting of "baits," considered labor-intensive and of limited use, and intensive summer fallowing. Loose soil provides the best habitat for the pale western cutworm, a native of the semi-arid regions and larval form of a moth. Even as late as 1926, entomologists knew of no effective means of control other than leaving fields undisturbed after August 1, thus preventing the adult moths from laying their eggs. This conflicted, of course, with other advice the farmers were receiving about the importance of fall cultivation. The western wheat-stem sawfly spread from its usual habitat of wild grasses to cultivated plants as settlement progressed. While reported at the turn of the century, it did not become a serious menace in southwestern Saskatchewan until the mid-1920s. Spring wheat was the crop most seriously affected. In 1931, the Department of Agriculture estimated provincial loss from these insects in the period 1926–31 in the region of $54 million. Invariably, the southwest corner of Saskatchewan was among those areas where these insects had damaged crops.

Better known than any of these insects, perhaps only because of its visibility, was the grasshopper. Several outbreaks in the mid-nineteenth century were so severe that observers described them in biblical terms. When Thomas Millman traveled through the south country with the British North American Boundary Commission in 1872, he said that grasshoppers "fairly blackened the sky."[14] It was not until 1918, however, that this pest seriously affected crops in southern Saskatchewan. In 1920 the government convened a conference of provincial and federal entomological authorities to prescribe a solution. It was there that they revealed the magnitude of the problem. Some 350,000 acres (141,640 ha) of cropland were affected in thirty-nine municipalities, extending from the Manitoba border and the international boundary in the southeast to Saskatoon in the northwest. They estimated that 21 percent of the crop, worth $1.7 million, had been destroyed despite poison campaigns.

From the start, the provincial Department of Agriculture viewed this campaign as a war. It amended the Rural Municipality Act to make it the duty of every council to purchase poison and ensure its use. It launched an extensive publicity campaign to inform farmers about the extent of the threat and appropriate means of dealing with it. Within the department, staff were assigned specifically to marshal the farm forces of the "Hopper Brigade." A director-general oversaw the campaign, a quartermaster distributed supplies, a chief field director supervised eighteen field directors, who in turn oversaw the work of four municipal captains. They enlisted school children as scouts. During the season, 7200 tons (6530 tonnes) of bait were distributed in the fields. Although the impact of the bait distribution remains uncertain, provincial authorities estimated that in 1920 the campaign resulted in the preservation of 1,400,000 acres (566,599 ha) of cropland, one-tenth of the provincial total, worth at least $25 million.

A Landscape of Utility

Reflecting on these agrarian interventions into the environment, we realize that we are looking at practical means to greater profit. Measures such as bait setting for gophers or weed control were remedies prescribed by scientific experts whose goal was enhanced farm productivity. They took their cue from politicians and administrators concerned above all else with provincial economic growth. Other matters, such as the extirpation of game and predators, were rooted firmly in a pervasive cult of domesticity that declared wild things to be valueless precisely because they were beyond the farmer's control. Given the difficulty of making this dry land produce cereal crops, the farmer's emphasis on managing the environment—by which we really mean attempting to eliminate or at least nullify the threat of any natural force or creature deemed inimical to the monoculture regime—is understandable. The undeniable hardships imposed by the environment, together with the glorious future it occasionally held out to those who tilled its soils, ensured that farmers were the least sentimental people ever to live in the southwest. In their ignorance, which was the ignorance of the times, they farmed a land that should never have known the power of the plow and in so doing they produced a legacy of environmental ruin.

By 1930, however, human modification of the environment in southwestern Saskatchewan had reached its zenith. In the decade of intense, lingering drought that followed—the infamous "Dirty Thirties"—the framework supporting the area's precarious grain economy weakened with frightening suddenness and then collapsed utterly. Living a tenuous existence even in flush times, few of these farmers could cope simultaneously with desiccating winds, rock-bottom grain prices, grasshopper invasions, and tenacious bill collectors. Some could not endure. One homesteader recalled that her husband "would sometimes put in 200 acres of crop, and a three-day blow would send the sand flying and cut off the small tender blades. He would then walk from window to window crying, with his lungs full of sand that he had breathed in while seeding."[15] He later committed suicide.

Unable to ride out the Great Depression, many farmers simply walked away from their considerable investment in land, buildings, livestock, and machinery. Between 1931 and 1941, nearly one-quarter of them relinquished their claims; by 1956, the decline in local farmers had reached 40 percent. Predictably, these were people who had been tilling some of the poorest soils in western Canada. Despite the great technological and scientific advances in cereal agriculture that occurred after the Second World War, the parched interior lands of the southwest never again saw farmers in such numbers. Now, most of the acreage that they abandoned as an economic wasteland is again carpeted with nutritious grass and grazed by livestock.

CONCLUSION
Culture and Environment

In the summer of 1874, George Dawson, working as a geologist with the British North American Boundary Commission, became the first scientist to document at first-hand deposits of lignite coal and dinosaur fossils in what later became known as southwestern Saskatchewan. It is perhaps fitting to invoke the example of a geologist as a preface to summarizing this examination of southwestern Saskatchewan history. Unlike their counterparts in other scientific disciplines, geologists must base their work on interpretation of events long past. They share with historians an inability to examine personally the changes they are investigating. Instead, they must seek repetitive patterns and compare those patterns with what they know of change elsewhere in the world. Examined in this way, the history of environmental change becomes in great measure a search for context, an analysis of the larger forces that produced the environment that we see before us today.

The relationship between people and their environment is reciprocal. Catastrophic events, such as the prolonged drought of 1918–22, not only reinforce our appreciation of nature's intractability in the face of our efforts to transform it, but also point to the depth of human ingenuity in mitigating the effect of such disasters. Historian William Cronon explains this dialectic in this way:

> Environment may initially shape the range of choices available to a people at a given moment, but then culture reshapes environment in responding to those choices. The reshaped environment presents a new set of possibilities for cultural reproduction, thus setting up a new cycle of mutual determination. Changes in the way people create and re-create their livelihood must be analyzed in terms of changes not only in their *social* relations but in their *ecological* ones as well.[1]

As Cronon points out, people are frequently so adept at modifying the environment to suit their cultural and economic imperatives, so good at imposing a human template on the land, that eventually we may lose sight of the original environment.

A moment's reflection suggests that this has been the experience of most of the Canadian plains. In three-quarters of a century—a single lifetime—the buffalo landscape that dominated the plains for millennia yielded to a simplified ecosystem devoted to monoculture production. This radical reordering of the environment occurred when the global market economy extended its reach to include the region's inhabitants. Capitalism, as the economic historian Karl Polanyi has explained, was marked by a shift in motive from that of subsistence to that of gain. This transition began in earnest on the Great Plains around the mid-nineteenth century and progressed through three main phases by 1930. Each phase turned on the harvest of a specific commodity for profit. Buffalo were the main commodity before 1880, domestic livestock from 1880 to 1908, and wheat from 1908 to 1930. Environmental alteration, characterized principally by a loss of ecological diversity, was apparent in all phases; only its intensity varied. Economically, the change represented the triumph of market capitalism; ecologically, it meant a stunning loss of natural diversity. Culturally, it meant recurrent social crisis.

Environmental changes, no less than religious upheavals or political movements or economic policies, are cultural phenomena. They reflect the values of the dominant society. In recounting as best we can the environmental history of any land we have inhabited, we sketch an image of our own evolution as a society. We expose our material priorities, our technological prowess, even our morality. When all is said and done, we reveal our human nature.

Endnotes

Notes to Introduction

1. Cronon, *Changes in the Land,* p. 13.
2. Wood Mountain Historical Society, *They Came to Wood Mountain.* See, for example, pp. 93, 94, 120, 132, and 138.
3. Cronon, *Changes in the Land,* p. 6.

Notes to Chapter One

1. Palliser, *Papers Relative to the Exploration by Captain Palliser,* p. 14.
2. Anderson, "The North-American Boundary from the Lakes of the Woods to the Rocky Mountains," pp. 250, 251.
3. Hewgill, "In the Days of Pioneering."
4. Featherstonhaugh, "Narrative of the Operations of the British North American Boundary Commission," p. 43.
5. Arthur, "An Introduction to the Ecology of Early Historic Communal Bison Hunting," p. 16.
6. Palliser, *Papers Relative to the Exploration by Captain Palliser*, p. 14.
7. Arthur, "An Introduction to the Ecology of Early Historic Communal Bison Hunting," p. 16.
8. *Opening Up the West,* p. 49.
9. Campbell and Twining, *Reports upon the Survey of the Boundary,* p. 282.
10. McEntyre, "Reminiscences," p. 9.
11. Wright, "Le Bois de Vache II," p. 227.
12. Dawson, "General Diary and Notebook."
13. Goudsblom, *Fire and Civilization,* p. 8.
14. Pyne, *Fire in America,* p. 81.
15. Gayton, *The Wheatgrass Mechanism,* p. 21.
16. Anderson, "The North-American Boundary," p. 245.
17. Dawson, *Report on the Exploration of the Country.*
18. Hewgill, "In the Days of Pioneering."
19. Cowie, *The Company of Adventurers,* p. 258.
20. Ibid., pp. 261, 262.
21. Palliser, *Papers Relative to the Exploration by Captain Palliser.*
22. Bell, "A Summer on the Plains," p. 16.

23. Cowie, *The Company of Adventurers,* pp. 303–04.
24. Featherstonhaugh, "Narrative of the Operations of the British North American Boundary Commission," p. 44.
25. Cowie, *The Company of Adventurers,* p. 290.
26. Ibid., p. 459.
27. Canada. Department of the Interior, *Annual Report for 1877.*
28. Campbell and Twining, *Reports Upon the Survey of the Boundary,* p. 63.
29. Ray, *Indians in the Fur Trade,* p. 185.
30. Cowie, *The Company of Adventurers,* p. 445.

Notes to Chapter Two

1. Kelsey, quoted in Warkentin, *The Western Interior of Canada,* pp. 23, 24.
2. James A. Walsh Papers, p. 25.
3. Kline, *Reminiscences.*
4. Cowie, *The Company of Adventurers,* p. 303.
5. Giraud, *The Metis in the Canadian West,* Volume 1, pp. 10, 11.
6. Dawson, "General Diary and Notebook."
7. Lestanc, "Souvenirs de 1860–1880," p. 24.
8. McDougall to Donald A. Smith, January 8, 1874.
9. Beal, Foster, and Zuk, "The Métis Hivernement Settlement," p. 82.
10. Milloy, *The Plains Cree,* p. 104.
11. Meredith, "Memorandum: Indian Policy in the North-West Territories."
12. "Petition of the Métis of Qu'Appelle," 1874.
13. Canada. Department of Indian Affairs, *Annual Report for 1880.*
14. Galt to Dewdney, March 22, 1880.
15. Dawson, "General Diary and Notebook," May 1874.
16. Anderson, "The North-American Boundary."
17. Stevens, "Narrative and Final Report of Explorations," p. 236.
18. Ibid., p. 111.
19. Palliser, quoted in Spry, *The Palliser Expedition,* p. 60.
20. Morton, *Henry Youle Hind,* pp. 69, 70.
21. Owram, *Promise of Eden,* p. 65.

Notes to Chapter Three

1. Quoted in Owram, *Promise of Eden,* p. 160.
2. Wood Mountain Historical Society, *They Came to Wood Mountain,* p. 32.
3. Canada. Department of the Interior, *Annual Report for 1886.*
4. Paul, *The Far West,* p. 202.
5. Canada. *Annual Report of the Commissioner of the North-West Mounted Police for 1888.*
6. Canada. *Annual Report of the Commissioner of the North-West Mounted Police for 1892.*

7.   Canada. *Annual Report of the Commissioner of the North-West Mounted Police for 1894.*

8.   Canada. *Annual Report of the Minister of Agriculture for 1896.*

9.   Canada. *Annual Report of the Commissioner of the North-West Mounted Police for 1897.*

10.   Jones to Sheperd, February 13, 1966.

11.   This statistical analysis is based on "Ranches in Saskatchewan in Existence 31st March 1912."

12.   Saskatchewan. Department of Agriculture, *Annual Report for 1909–10.*

13.   Canada. *Annual Report of the Commissioner of the Royal North-West Mounted Police for 1912.*

14.   Healy to Mantle, November 27, 1913.

15.   Saskatchewan. Department of Agriculture, "(Final) Report of Live Stock Commission," p. 313.

16.   Saskatchewan. Department of Agriculture, *Annual Report for 1918.*

17.   Long, *The Great Canadian Range,* p. 64.

18.   Ibid., p. 171.

Notes to Chapter Four

1.   Nominal Rolls for West Assiniboia, Swift Current Part 2.

2.   Otterson, "Thirty Years Ago on the Whitemud River," p. 16.

3.   Canada. *Annual Report of the Commissioner of the North-West Mounted Police for 1880.*

4.   Long, *70 Years a Cowboy,* p. 9.

5.   Goudie, *The Human Impact on the Natural Environment,* pp. 34, 35.

6.   Stinton address, 1908.

7.   Miles, "General Survey Report."

8.   Rowe and Coupland, "Vegetation of the Canadian Plains," p. 243.

9.   *Management of Prairie Rangeland,* p. 19.

10.   "An Ordinance for the Prevention of Prairie and Forest Fires."

11.   Canada. *Annual Report of the Commissioner of the North-West Mounted Police for 1888.*

12.   Canada. Department of the Interior, *Annual Report for 1894.*

13.   Canada. *Annual Report of the Minister of Agriculture for 1897.*

14.   Commissioner of Agriculture to His Honour The Lieutenant Governor in Council, January 10, 1898.

15.   "Wolf Bounty Returns."

16.   Saskatchewan. Department of Agriculture, *Annual Report for 1914.*

17.   Wood Mountain Historical Society, *They Came to Wood Mountain,* p. 176.

Notes to Chapter Five

1. Saskatchewan. *Report of the Royal Commission Inquiry into Farming Conditions,* 1921, p. 8.
2. Canada. Department of the Interior, *Annual Report for 1908.*
3. Saskatchewan. Department of Agriculture, *Annual Report for 1906.*
4. Cowper, "General Survey Report."
5. Smith testimony, 1930.
6. Greenlay interview, 1993.
7. Wood Mountain Historical Society, *They Came to Wood Mountain,* p. 195.
8. Saskatchewan. *Report of the Royal Commission Inquiry into Farming Conditions, 1921,* p. 35.
9. Ibid., p. 36.
10. Anderson, *A History of Soil Erosion by Wind,* p. 8.
11. Bracken, "Soil Drifting in Western Canada," July 1920.
12. Kraenzel, *The Great Plains in Transition,* p. 19.
13. Bennett, *Northern Plainsmen,* p. 229.
14. Miles, "General Survey Report," February 1, 1911.
15. Saskatchewan. Department of Agriculture, *Annual Report for 1914.*
16. Saskatchewan. Department of Agriculture, *Annual Report for 1920.*
17. Saskatchewan. Department of Agriculture, *Annual Report for 1911.*
18. Scott Papers, "Better Farming Train."
19. Saskatchewan. Department of Agriculture, *Annual Report for 1920.*

Notes to Chapter Six

1. Walker to the Deputy Minister, Department of Agriculture, Regina, February 8, 1921.
2. Saskatchewan. Department of Agriculture, *Annual Report for 1921.*
3. Saskatchewan Stockgrowers' Association, "Statement of Facts Governing the Ranching Industry."
4. *Manitoba Free Press,* "What Is to Be Done With Our Dry Areas?" September 5, 1919, p. 1.
5. Cory to Martin, February 21, 1921.
6. Saskatchewan. *Report of the Royal Commission Inquiry into Farming Conditions, 1921,* p. 51.
7. Ibid.
8. Ibid., p. 55.
9. Saskatchewan. Department of Agriculture, *Annual Report for 1921.*
10. Saskatchewan. Department of Agriculture, *Annual Report for 1924.*
11. Campbell, *Swift Current Research Station,* p. 1.
12. These and the following characterizations about farming in the southwest during the 1920s are based on statistical analysis of provincial and federal censuses and Department of Agriculture annual reports.

13.   Pohlman, "Testimony before the Royal Commission on Immigration and Settlement, 1930."

Notes to Chapter Seven

1.   Saskatchewan. *Report of the Royal Commission Inquiry into Farming Conditions,* 1921, p. 46.
2.   Haughton, *Green Immigrants.*
3.   "Wood Mountain Agency—Coal Mining Location on the Wood Mountain Reserve."
4.   Saskatchewan. Department of Agriculture, *Annual Report for 1907.*
5.   Saskatchewan. Department of Agriculture, *Annual Report for 1913.*
6.   Ibid.
7.   Saskatchewan. Department of Agriculture, *Annual Report for 1916.*
8.   Saskatchewan. Department of Agriculture, *Annual Report for 1913.*
9.   This is the title of a 1930 Imperial Oil Limited booklet on weed control written for farm children by Duncan Marshall, Alberta's minister of Agriculture.
10.   Saskatchewan. Department of Agriculture, *Annual Report for 1905.*
11.   Crosby, *Ecological Imperialism,* p. 149.
12.   Saskatchewan. Department of Agriculture, *Annual Report for 1915.*
13.   Clark and Fletcher, *Farm Weeds of Canada,* p. 8.
14.   Millman, "Impressions of the West in the Early 'Seventies."
15.   Moorhouse, *Buffalo Horn Valley School District No. 930,* p. 31.

Notes to Conclusion

1.   Cronon, *Changes in the Land,* p. 13.

Paul, Rodmond W. *The Far West and the Great Plains in Transition, 1859–1900*. New York: Harper & Row, 1988.

Peel, Bruce Braden. "R.M. 45: The Social History of a Rural Municipality (Mankota)." M.A. Thesis, University of Saskatchewan, 1946.

Perren, Richard. "The North American Beef and Cattle Trade with Great Britain, 1870–1914." *Economic History Review* 2nd Series, 24 (1971): 430–44.

"Petition from Fort Qu'Appelle Metis regarding hunting and trading rights to the west and south-west of Qu'Appelle." Canada. Sessional Papers. *Annual Report of the Department of the Interior for 1874*.

Pohlman, F. W. "F. W. Pohlman, Secretary of Grassy Lake Rural Municipality, Testimony Before the Royal Commission on Immigration and Settlement, 1930." R249.V29. Saskatchewan Archives Board (Regina).

Pyne, Stephen. *Fire in America: A Cultural History of Wildland and Rural Fire*. Princeton: Princeton University Press, 1982.

Raby, S. "Prairie Fires in the North-West." *Saskatchewan History* 19, no. 3 (1966): 81–99.

"Ranches in Saskatchewan in Existence 31st March 1912." Clippings File on Ranches and Ranching. Saskatchewan Archives Board (Regina).

Ray, Arthur J. *Indians in the Fur Trade: Their Role as Hunters, Trappers and Middlemen in the Lands Southwest of Hudson Bay, 1660–1870*. Toronto: University of Toronto Press, 1974.

Rondeau, L'Abbé C. *La Montagne de Bois (Willow-Bunch, Sask.)*. Quebec: L'Édition Sociale, 1923.

Rowe, J. Stan. "Lightning Fires in Saskatchewan Grassland." *Canadian Field Naturalist* 83, no. 4 (October–December 1969): 317–24.

Rowe, J. Stan, and Robert T. Coupland. "Vegetation of the Canadian Plains." *Prairie Forum* 9, no. 2 (Fall 1986): 231–48.

Saskatchewan. *Final Report of the Live Stock Commission of the Province of Saskatchewan, 1918*. Regina: King's Printer, 1918.

———. *Interim Report of the Live Stock Commission of the Province of Saskatchewan*. Regina: King's Printer, 1917.

Saskatchewan. *Report of the Royal Commission Inquiry into Farming Conditions, 1921*.

———. Department of Agriculture. *Annual Reports,* various years.

Saskatchewan Stockgrowers' Association. "Statement of Facts Governing the Ranching Industry in Western Canada; Prepared by the Delegates Appointed by the Western Stock-Growers Protective Association, and the Interior Stock Association of British Columbia for the Information of the Hon. Minister of the Interior for Canada," 1921. R261.II, Subfile 12. Saskatchewan Archives Board (Regina).

Scott, Walter. Walter Scott Papers. "Better Farming Train." 1915. R7.1. Reel 13. Saskatchewan Archives Board (Regina).

Smith, Al. "Testimony, Royal Commission on Immigration and Settlement (Saskatchewan), 1930." R249.V28. Saskatchewan Archives Board (Regina).

Spector, David. *Agriculture on the Prairies, 1870–1940*. Ottawa: Environment Canada, 1983.

Spry, Irene M. *The Palliser Expedition: An Account of John Palliser's British North American Exploring Expedition, 1857–1860.* Reprint, Saskatoon, SK: Fifth House, 1995.

Stevens, Isaac I. "Narrative and Final Report of Explorations for a Route for a Pacific Railroad Near the 47th and 49th Parallels of North Latitude from St. Paul to Puget Sound." In *Reports of Explorations and Surveys to Ascertain the Most Practicable and Economical Route for a Railroad from the Mississippi River to the Pacific Ocean, 1853–55*, Volume XII, Book I. Washington: Thomas H. Ford, 1860.

Stinton, Robert. "Address Delivered by Robert Stinton, President, Saskatchewan Stock Breeders' Association, at the General Convention of the National Live Stock Association Held at Ottawa, February 5, 6 and 7, 1908." R276.II.1. Saskatchewan Archives Board (Regina).

Thompson, John H. *The Harvests of War: The Prairie West, 1914–1918.* Toronto: McClelland and Stewart, 1978.

Tinkham, W. A. "A Report on the Reconnaissance of the Three Buttes." In *Pacific Railroad Report of Explorations and Surveys to Ascertain the Most Practicable and Economical Route for a Railroad from the Mississippi River to the Pacific Ocean, 1853–55,* Volume XII. Washington: Thomas H. Ford, 1860.

Turner, A. R. "The Journal of George M. Dawson, 1873." *Saskatchewan History* 21, no. 1 (Winter 1968): 1–23.

Turner. A. R. "Motherwell and Agricultural Education, 1905–1918." *Saskatchewan History* 12 (August 1959): 81–96.

Waiser, W. A. "A Willing Scapegoat: John Macoun and the Route of the CPR." *Prairie Forum* 10, no. 1 (Spring 1985): 65–82.

Walker, W. H. "W. H. Walker to the Deputy Minister, Department of Agriculture, Regina." February 8, 1921. R261.XXIII.1. Saskatchewan Archives Board (Regina).

Walsh, James A. James A. Walsh Papers. M705. Provincial Archives of Manitoba.

Warkentin, John, editor. *The Western Interior of Canada: A Record of Geographical Discovery, 1612–1917.* Toronto: McClelland and Stewart, 1964.

Watts, F. B. *The Natural Vegetation of the Southern Great Plains of Canada.* Geographical Bulletin 41. Ottawa: Canada, Department of Mines and Technical Surveys, 1960.

White, Richard. *Land Use, Environment, and Social Change: The Shaping of Island County, Washington.* Seattle: University of Washington Press, 1980.

"Wolf Bounty Returns, 1901–1911." Record Book 13. Livestock Branch. AG.2.13. Saskatchewan Archives Board (Regina).

"Wood Mountain Agency—Coal Mining Location on the Wood Mountain Reserve, 1915–1949." RG 10, Volume 7462, File 18137, Part 1 (Reel C-14,764). National Archives Canada.

Wood Mountain Historical Society. *They Came to Wood Mountain.* Wood Mountain: Wood Mountain Historical Society, 1967.

Worster, Donald. "Cowboy Ecology." In *Under Western Skies: Nature and History in the American West*, edited by Donald Worster, pp. 34–52. New York: Oxford University Press, 1992.

―――. "Grassland Follies: Agricultural Capitalism on the Plains." In *Under Western Skies: Nature and History in the American West*, edited by Donald Worster, pp. 93–105. New York: Oxford University Press, 1992.

Wright, Milt. "Le Bois de Vache II: This Chip's for You Too." In *Buffalo*, edited by John E. Foster, Dick Harrison, and I. S. MacLaren, pp. 225–44. Edmonton: University of Alberta Press, 1992.

Index

If you enjoyed this book, read

The Cypress Hills: The Land and Its People

At the western edge of the grasslands are the Cypress Hills. In this book, authors Walter Hildebrandt and Brian Hubner tell a fascinating story about the Cypress Hills. They explain why those Hills—a 2600 square kilometre plateau straddling the Alberta/Saskatchewan/U.S. border—were an important gathering place for Aboriginal Peoples for thousands of years, and why the Canadian government did not want them there. The Indians and Métis came because game and lodge pole pine were plentiful. Buffalo abounded, and the authors describe all aspects of the buffalo hunt, from spiritual preparation to the final kill. Fur traders and wolfers came too— mostly from Montana—and with them clashes between the different worlds, leading to the 1873 Cypress Hills massacre. That event brough the North-West Mounted Police and led to the building of Fort Walsh in the Hills. It was in these Hills that Chief Sitting Bull and the Dakotas sought refuge after defeating Custer at the Battle of Little Big Horn. While the North-West Mounted Police worked to maintain peace, they also helped disperse Aboriginal Peoples from the area. As a result, today there is only one Indian reserve in the Cypress Hills area.

To order a copy of *The Cypress Hills,* send $21.40 (this total includes $3.50 shipping and handling and $1.40 GST) to:

Purich Publishing
Box 23032, Market Mall Post Office
Saskatoon, SK
Canada S7J 5H3

or ask at your bookstore.